Virgil's
Eclogues

Virgil's
Eclogues

TRANSLATED BY
Len Krisak

INTRODUCTION BY
Gregson Davis

PENN

University of Pennsylvania Press

Philadelphia

Latin text from P. Vergili Maronis, *Opera*, edited by R. A. B. Mynors,
Eclogues, pp. 1–28 (Oxford: Oxford University Press, 1969).
Reprinted by permission of Oxford University Press.

Published by
University of Pennsylvania Press
Philadelphia, Pennsylvania 19104-4112

Printed in the United States of America on acid-free paper
10 9 8 7 6 5 4 3 2 1

A Cataloging-in-Publication Data Record is available
from the Library of Congress
ISBN 978-0-8122-4225-6

CONTENTS

INTRODUCTION

THE TRIO OF MASTERPIECES THAT VIRGIL COMPOSED during the prolonged sunset of the Roman Republic[1] begins with the collection of ten poems that we have come to know by the conventional title *Eclogues* ("Selections"). Though these exquisite short poems inaugurate the sequence that continues with the *Georgics* and culminates in the *Aeneid*, they are neither less elegant in style nor less profound in philosophical insight than the later, more extensive works.

The book of *Eclogues* appeared on the scene approximately seven years before the decisive naval battle of Actium in 30 B.C.E. Octavian's triumph over Antony and Cleopatra in that contest brought the protracted Civil Wars to a close—an era scarred by radical social and political upheavals. The violent disintegration of the political fabric of the Republic had occasioned widespread anxiety among all sectors of society, and the establishment of a stable peace—the *pax Augusta*—was yet to materialize. An acute awareness of the disruption of the sociopolitical order is refracted through the artistic prism of the *Eclogues*. Their youthful author, who was to breathe new life into the Hellenistic genre of bucolic poetry, had very recently emerged from philosophical studies in an Epicurean "school" centered in the Bay of Naples, where Greek teachers such as Philodemus and Siro counted the Roman poets Horace and Varius among their associates and pupils.[2]

Virgil is a poet of ideas. Like his close friend, Horace, he thought deeply about the philosophical prerequisites for attaining inner tranquility, and about the limits on the human capacity to cope with extremes of adversity. He consistently explored these issues through the medium of poetry in all three of the major genres in which he worked: bucolic, didactic, and epic. While the traces of a deep philosophical *Bildung* are manifest throughout his poetic œuvre, these need to be extrapolated, in the case of the bucolic poems, from the conversations among his poet-herdsmen. At the same time, such extrapolations should not be guided by a desire to confine the various and sometimes competing worldviews expressed obliquely in the poems to the dogmas of any particular school.

When Virgil eventually composed the prologue to his magisterial epic, the *Aeneid*, he famously foregrounded the question of the nature of the Olympian gods in his idiosyncratic variation on the epic invocation of the muse: "Can anger so intense possess the minds of gods?" ("tantaene animis caelestibus irae?" *Aeneid* 1.11). The rhetorical interrogation represents a startling new note in the discourse of epic prologues, but it would be a mistake to suppose that Virgil's interest in such ethical paradoxes made its first appearance in the opening lines of the *Aeneid*. It is a regrettable aspect of the reception of the *Eclogues* that the prevailing orthodoxy tends to treat the collection as lightweight and charming verse, while their philosophical underpinnings have by and large retreated to the margins of critical exegesis. The *Eclogues* are in desperate need of rescue from centuries of trivialization of their intellectual content.

The *Eclogues* have been conventionally assigned to the genre of the "pastoral." As a few perceptive critics have noted,[3] however, the label is misleading on several nontrivial counts, for the complex of traits that came to define the pastoral tradition in later European literature is only superficially connected with Virgilian bucolic. It would be no exaggeration to state that the post-Virgilian pastoral genre (if we set aside the later Latin practitioners of the imperial period, such as Calpurnius Siculus and Nemesianus), which properly begins in the Italian Renaissance, is tangential in many important respects to the Roman poet's transmutation of Hellenistic bucolic poetry. A less anachronistic nomenclature for the genre would be the older term, "bucolic," which connects the Virgilian generic inflection with a dominant subgroup of poems in the corpus of the Greek Hellenistic poet Theocritus. Virgil's book of *Eclogues* harks back to, and transforms, Theocritean bucolic verse, but in opening up a new space within the earlier Greek genre it does not, as is still commonly repeated in the standard commentaries, sponsor an idealized, utopian "Arcadia" that is the stuff of later European poets and critics alike.

Let us engage in a round of timely iconoclasm about the nature of Virgil's Arcadia. In blatant contradistinction to a world of utopian fantasy and escapist bliss, the world of the *Eclogues* is permeated through and through with portrayals of human infelicity, catastrophic loss, and emotional turbulence. The defining tenor of these poetic sketches is a profound anxiety about the human capacity to cope with misfortune. A cursory review of the dominant themes of the ten poems in the cycle makes it ineluctably clear that Virgil's primary concern is with the world of human misery rather than with frivolous escapist constructions of an alternative universe purified of anguish and angst. A brief poem by poem synopsis of the predominant themes of Virgilian bucolic will be an instructive exercise.

The opening programmatic Eclogue juxtaposes a herdsman who is currently experiencing good fortune (Tityrus) with one who is a recent victim of misfortune (Meliboeus). The latter is in deep distress after having been dispossessed of his farm, while the former has had his plot restored following a presumed dispossession. At the conclusion of their exchange, the fortunate herdsman offers consolation to

his despondent interlocutor in the form of an invitation to share a
meal in his humble abode. Tityrus carefully contextualizes his present felicity at more than one juncture in the course of the dialogue: he
explains to Meliboeus that it is contingent on the disposition of a divine benefactor and, more important, that his life has in the past been
subject to vicissitude. E.2 is an anguished monologue chanted by a
herdsman whose love is unreciprocated and who eventually manages
to place a limit (*modus*) on his torment by recognizing his pathologi-
cal condition (*dementia*) through the exercise of singing ("O Corydon,
O Corydon! What *is* this madness?").[4] The third poem in the series
exposes the emotional underbelly of the herdsmens' interpersonal
relations. In the succinct formulation of Guy Lee, the author of the
Penguin bilingual edition of the *Eclogues*: "Two shepherds meet and
taunt each other with accusations of theft, sexual perversion, mali-
cious damage to property, jealousy and musical incompetence."[5] This
accurate précis hardly amounts to a portrayal of utopian bliss.

The fourth Eclogue, which has earned the sobriquet "Messianic"
because of its reference to a miraculous child (*puer*) and a virgin (famously misread in the Medieval period as a prophecy of the birth
of Christ), heralds the dawn of a renewed Golden Age, but its account of the Four Ages draws on a fundamental model of cyclicality.
Virgil's language is unambiguous about the nonlinear nature of the
sequence of cosmic ages bearing the iconic metal tropes Gold, Silver,
Bronze, and Iron. The parade of ages may, with no loss of precision,
be characterized as "vicissitude writ large." What is more, there is no
clean break between the recycled ages: traces (*vestigia*) of the crime-
ridden Iron Age, for instance, overlap with the commencement of the
Golden, which is destined in the grand scheme of things to give way
in its turn to Silver. The notion that the Golden Age prognosticated
by the speaker of E.4 is to be conceived as a stable paradisiacal order
is an importation from later Christian belief in a unilinear diachronic

progression towards an eternal divine kingdom—a conception deeply incongruent with the ancient Indo-European myth of a recurrent cosmic cycle of ages.

To continue our catalogue of themes: the poem that occupies the midpoint in the sequence (*E.*5) contains two complementary encomia of the legendary founder of bucolic poetry, the figure of Daphnis; but the first opens with an agonized lament for "the cruel death Daphnis died." His subsequent apotheosis, the reward for his musical reputation, is enunciated by the second singer, Mopsus, as consolation for his catastrophic decline into disfavor after his semi-divine lover, a nymph, brutally avenges her sexual betrayal. Such eternal felicity as is eventually experienced by this prototype of the bucolic poet-herdsman takes place in his post-terrestrial afterlife as a constellation.

The sixth Eclogue opens with a proem that is appropriately programmatic with respect to both style and theme, since it inaugurates the second half of the collection. In regard to theme, which is the subject of this synopsis, the role of the embedded poet-philosopher is played by the Dionysian figure of Silenus, who unfolds a panoramic history that is predominantly (though not exclusively) a catalogue of disastrous events, several of them featuring the destructive effects of erotic passion. On the positive side, he mentions the renewal of the human race after Jupiter's wrathful punishment in the form of the flood, as well as a previous iteration of the Golden Age during the mythical reign of Saturn. Conspicuous among the lugubrious tales he outlines (which receive greater elaboration than the semi-felicitous ones) are the fates of the hapless Pasiphae, who mated with a bull; Hylas, the favorite of Heracles, who was accidentally left behind in the course of the Argonautic expedition; Scylla, daughter of Nisus, turned into a hideous monster after a disastrous love experience; and Philomela, victim of rape on the part of the sadistic Tereus, who came to a macabre and gruesome end. According to the account of Silenus, the journey of

humankind from creation to the present can scarcely be described as a
master narrative with a happy ending.

The next Eclogue in the series takes the form of a bucolic singing match between two "Arcadian" master-musicians, Corydon and
Thyrsis. The contest is a strenuously performed "amoebean" exchange
that is a far cry in tone from the amicable swap of eulogies that we
heard in *E.5* (devoted, as we have noted, to the theme of the death
and apotheosis of Daphnis). Thyrsis, in particular, often strikes a dis-
tinctly invidious note in his quatrains, resorting in several instances
to gratuitous detraction rather than celebration. His much-debated
failure in the contest (the judge awards the palm to Corydon at the
end of the poem) is probably attributable to his jaundiced worldview,
as opposed to some identifiable inferiority of technique. In the eighth
Eclogue we are treated to yet another variant on the bucolic *agon* in
which two rival singers vie in less than friendly terms in the arena of
(un)success in love. The portrayal of erotic relationships that emerges
in the course of the poem is in tune with the norms of Greco-Roman
love poetry, where reciprocity of affection is seldom assured and celebration of felicitous outcomes is relatively rare. Thus the first singer,
Damon, commences the exchange with a moribund *cri de coeur*:

> Lucifer, rise. You bring the world its living light,
> While I, deceived in faithless love by Nysa, my
> Betrothed, complain. And though the gods have never helped,
> I call on them, as in my final hour, I die. (8:17–20)

He goes on to utter invidious sentiments, such as the following:

> Now Nysa marries Mopsus? Lovers, what to think!
> We'll soon see griffins mate with mares; in days to come,
> The timid deer will join with hunting dogs to drink. (26–28)

When the second singer, Alphesiboeus, takes up the challenge, we are treated to a prolonged account of magic ritual (words and actions) intended to bind the beloved to the will of the lover. Reciprocity is here a desperate wish on the part of the singer, and the outcome of the magic spells and rites turns out to be ambiguous, for at the conclusion of the poem Virgil raises the question of whether the favorable result of magical practices in an erotic context is a wish-fulfillment fantasy:

> Look there! All by themselves, while I was dawdling, embers
> Have blown; the shrine is licked by flame. A sign, from sparks!
> Surely there's *something*: Hylax in the doorway barks.
> Could it be true? *Or are such dreams all lovers' own?*
>
> (108–9; translator's emphasis)

The penultimate Eclogue explores the issue of the efficacy of poetry as consolation for misfortune. The subject is broached in the opening lines, in which we are told that the singer, Moeris, has lost his small farm in the land redistributions in the aftermath of the Civil Wars. Clearly we are meant to recall the analogous fate of Meliboeus in the first Eclogue, but in this iteration what is foregrounded is the mitigating role of poetry in the face of catastrophic loss. In the Virgilian dialogue, Lycidas asks Moeris to verify the rumor that the lands in question had been preserved through the power of Menalcas' song. To this naïve and wistful inquiry, Moeris replies:

> You did; that's how the rumor ran. But Lycidas,
> In Mars's weaponed world, our songs prevail the way
> Chaonian doves do with the eagle in a fray. (9:11–15)

Moeris's position on the limits of art corresponds with the view of W. H. Auden as articulated in the poem, "In Memory of W. B. Yeats":

For poetry makes nothing happen: it survives
In the valley of its making where executives
would never want to tamper...[6]

Confronted with the brutal confiscation of their lands, Virgil's
singers have recourse to the task of memory in preserving the trans-
mitted poetic tradition. Verbal art itself escapes the destruction that
is inherent in the material order through the continual recall and re-
performance of bucolic poetry—including examples of Virgil's own
compositions, which are cited in this poem by their first lines. The
function of recollection via poetic performance, however, is not to in-
dulge in nostalgia for a utopian fantasy, but rather to preserve art as
an antidote to the vagaries of fortune.

The tenth and final Eclogue features the unhappy love life of Virgil's close friend and fellow-poet Cornelius Gallus, the founder of the
genre of Latin elegiac poetry. In the persona of the poet enslaved to
love for a capricious mistress, Gallus reenters the rural stage with the
forlorn hope of sharing in the imagined felicity of the bucolic world.
In the process he learns that neither reciprocal love nor consolation
for his plight is forthcoming as a result of this excursion into another
generic terrain. On the contrary, he comes to the disillusioned realiza-
tion that Amor is a divinity whose dominion in not subject to human
manipulation or control. He is eventually obliged to relinquish his
fantasy-projection of bucolic salvation and resign himself to the rig-
ors of erotic experience:

Love conquers all. Let Love then smile at our defeat. (10:69)

In light of this thematic (and, I hope, revisionist) overview, it is
legitimate to ask, "Does the myth of Virgil's rose-tinted Arcadia find
justification in the text?" As far as internal evidence from the poems

themselves is concerned, it can most certainly be traced to a common misinterpretation of the programmatic first Eclogue. As we have noted fleetingly above, it is the hapless Meliboeus who projects onto Tityrus the view that the latter's present felicity is destined to be irreversible. Meliboeus continues to project this rosy picture of Tityrus' future even though the fortunate herdsman had carefully qualified his situation by describing his past infelicity and by making it clear that his own continued good fortune is contingent on the good graces of a beneficent god. Despite these corrections to his fantasy, Meliboeus persists in projecting a future of unalloyed bliss for his interlocutor:

> Old man, you're lucky. Here, amid familiar brooks
> And sacred springs, you'll search out cool, refreshing shade.
> And near your neighbor's boundary, as it always did,
> The hedge that keeps the bees of Hybla willow-fed
> Will often lull you to your sleep with soft susurrus.
> Below the bluff, a pruner tunes the air with airs,
> While all along, the doves who are your special care
> Coo with the moaning doves in immemorial elms. (1:51–58)

Against this picture of unchanging future bliss in a *locus amoenus*, Tityrus had earlier emphasized his own past vicissitudes in regard to both his love affairs and his sociopolitical status. In short, the overconfident assertion of an ideal future existence for Tityrus is pronounced by the disillusioned persona in the dialogue, who sees his own current misfortune as irreversible as he heads off into exile at the ends of the civilized world. The subjectivity of Meliboeus' position—the presumption that both his own infelicity and Tityrus's felicity are irreversible—is a very flimsy platform on which to erect the widespread misconception that the *Eclogues* as a whole reflect an idyllic existence removed from deep human problems and anxieties.

Bucolic poetry relies on a conventional scaffolding of singer-herds-men in dialogue. I have deliberately used the term "singer-herdsmen" rather than "herdsmen-singers," for the priority of poetry-making over tending flocks that is mirrored in my preferred hyphenation cannot be too prominently marked. This priority is critical to the poetics of the genre as practiced both by its founder, the Hellenistic Greek poet Theocritus, and by its superlative Roman exponent Virgil. Although the adjective "bucolic" is derived from a Greek word denoting "cowherd," the protagonists who populate the bucolic landscape comprise herds-men of varied stripe (goatherds and shepherds as well as cowherds). Already in the Theocritean corpus the synecdochic status of the cow-herd as an over-arching trope for a certain type of singer becomes transparent. In a salient metaphor he employs in the final lines of *Idyll* 11, which recounts the unhappy love of the Cyclops, Theocritus encap-sulates the primacy of singing over herding in the universe of bucolic:

Thus did Polyphemus *shepherd* his love with minstrelsy.[7]

I have glanced in summary fashion at major aspects of the ideation-al content of bucolic discourse. By way of conclusion, a few remarks about Virgilian style are in order—particularly so in the context of this introduction to an English translation of the *Eclogues*. In seeking a literary-historical frame for understanding the stylistic register of bucolic poetry, we can do no better that to follow the cues inserted in the prologue to *E*.6:

She never blushed at woodland living—not my Muse—
For Thalia first approved of verse from Syracuse.
But when I sang of royal broils, the Cynthian tugged
My ear and counseled: "Tityrus, a shepherd ought
To feed sheep fat, but sing a song that's spun out thin." (6:1–5)

The name Tityrus here stands for the aspiring bucolic poet, and the staged intervention by the god Apollo is a standard motif in conventional disclaimers of high style on the part of Alexandrian poets and their Latin imitators. Ancient poets themselves, no less than their contemporary theorists, adhered by and large to the principle of "stylistic decorum"—the fundamental premise of which is that registers of style should correlate with levels of subject matter. Leading Latin poets of the late Republic (the amatory elegists, Tibullus, Propertius, and Ovid, as well as the practitioners of other lyric genres, such as Horace) frequently incorporated their choice of generic register into the fabric of their verse. Such performed choices involved disavowal of other genres (the so-called *recusatio*).[8] The rhetorical function of such formal disavowals is to carve out a stylistic "space" for the poem at hand. In the prologue to *E*.6, which, as is well known, is beholden to the Alexandrian aesthetics of the short poem, Virgil is at pains to prepare the reader to apprehend the intermediary register he is about to adopt—an idiosyncratic space between the grandiloquent speech of epic and tragedy and the lowly conversational tone of comedy.

Though the diction of Virgilian bucolic eschews the grand manner, it hardly ever descends to the level of the colloquial. As the late Wendell Clausen remarks in the introduction to his commentary: "Ancient pastoral poetry, the poetry of Theocritus and Virgil, is never simple, though it affects to be; and in this affectation of simplicity, the disparity between the meanness of its subject and the refinement of the poet's art, lies the essence of pastoral."[9] The refined style to which Clausen here alludes resonates, at the acoustic level, with musical performance. Vowel notes that are mimetic of reed pipes are heard in the very first overture of the *Eclogues*. Len Krisak's rendition of this iconic prelude seeks to imitate the melodic virtuosity of the original:

Tityre tu patulae recubans sub tegmine fagi
siluestrem tenui Musam meditaris auena;
nos patriae finis et dulcia linquimus arua.
nos patriam fugimus; tu, Tityre, lentus in umbra
formosam resonare doces Amaryllida silvas. (1:1–5)

Under a beech's stretching branches, there you lie,
Tityrus, trying, on the slimmest reed, to court
The forest muse, while I must leave, saying good-bye
To home, with its dear fields. But you, in shady ease,
Make "Lovely Amaryllis" echo through the trees.

The translations in this volume succeed in achieving the all-important musicality of effect, while sustaining a delicate balance between the pedestrian and the formal, the mundane and the sublime—the style that his fellow poet Horace famously characterized as "molle atque facetum" ("refined and witty"). The reader who is attuned to the unparalleled tonalities of Virgilian *melos* will find many felicitous renditions of the Latin maestro in this fresh new translation of a lyric masterpiece.

TRANSLATOR'S PREFACE

The translators, men and women, sit in their cells /
and make honey...

   —Yehuda Amichai, *Open Closed Open*

C OMING TO THE TRANSLATION OF VIRGIL'S *ECLOGUES*
(the Greek word means "choices" or "selections," which may
explain why the more descriptive *Bucolics* is often favored), I
determined to set myself only a few criteria (though not necessarily
here in descending order of importance): accuracy, sensitivity to the
spirit and tone of the work insofar as I could determine them, ap-
proximation in English accentual-syllabic equivalents to the quantita-
tive Latin meter,[1] and—perhaps quixotically—quality as a poem in
English.

This last standard often appears in other Virgilian translators' ac-
counts of their work lightly disguised as an effort to "produce a poem
that sounds like something Virgil might write in English were he alive
today."[2] I am afraid this is miles beyond my capabilities, assuming I
were able to imagine what such a work might sound like in the first
place. I strove instead to give Virgil as much music in English as I
felt his poems possessed in Latin. This should help to explain, if not
entirely justify, an abundant use of alliteration, assonance, consonance,

rhyme, and syntactical figuration—what philologists and linguists call *marked language*. Occasionally, the well-intentioned impertinence of a deliberate echo from well-known poems in English surfaces. I can defend these only as expressions of the ebullient spirits of a versifier grateful in the extreme to Milton, Tennyson, Auden, and others. Perhaps Christopher Ricks's masterful work *Allusion to the Poets* may help to explain the spirit in which these borrowings appear.

By and large, though, such playful moments are never offered to the reader at the expense of the Latin. I have tried to make this translation so much a line-for-line version as to enable the student reader in search of a key proper noun to find the term no more than a line away from the corresponding Latin line in any given instance. How successful that endeavor, I leave to the reader.

...

I have followed the Oxford edition included in this volume with the exception of two lines:

At *E*. 1.65, my translation, "Some, Scythia or the Oaxes, sluicing Crete," is from_____

At *E*. iv.62, my translation, "Nor gods board one—on whom his parents have not smiled," is from the Latin "cui non risere parentes."

...

Eclogues vi and ix first appeared in *PNReview 180* (34, no. 4) (March/April 2008).

...

Finally, all translation is compromise—as the American scholar-poet J. V. Cunningham might have put it, a series of exclusions.

The Eclogues

ECLOGA I

Meliboeus:

Tityre, tu patulae recubans sub tegmine fagi
silusetrem tenui Musam meditaris auena;
nos patriae finis et dulcia linquimus arua.
nos patriam fugimus; tu, Tityre, lentus in umbra
formosam resonare doces Amaryllida siluas.   5

Tityrus:

O Meliboee, deus nobis haec otia fecit.
namque erit ille mihi semper deus, illius aram
saepe tener nostris ab ouilibus imbuet agnus.
ille meas errare boues, ut cernis, et ipsum
ludere quae uellem calamo permisit agresti.   10

M:

Non equidem inuideo, miror magis; undique totis
usque adeo turbatur agris. en ipse capellas
protinus aeger ago; hanc etiam uix, Tityre, duco.
hic inter densas corylos modo namque gemellos,
spem gregis, a! silice in nuda conixa reliquit.   15
saepe malum hoc nobis, si mens non laeua fuisset,
de caelo tactas memini praedicere quercus.
sed tamen iste deus qui sit, da, Tityre, nobis.

ECLOGUE I

Meliboeus:

Under a beech's stretching branches, there you lie,
Tityrus, trying, on the slimmest reed, to court
The forest muse, while I must leave, saying good-bye
To home, with its dear fields. But you, in shady ease,
Make "Lovely Amaryllis" echo through the trees.   5

Tityrus:

Well, Meliboeus, one who's like a god to me
Gave me this peace. His altar stone will always be
Bloodstained from spring lambs barely in the pen a day,
Because he lets my cattle roam, as you can see,
And lets me play my panpipe—any melody.   10

M:

I'm far less jealous than amazed, my friend. The land
Is crying havoc, and I'm sick at heart, for driving
My goats just now, I couldn't budge this nanny caught
In hazel thickets, struggling as twins were arriving.
She dropped the future of the flock on naked flint!   15
I would have realized the signs had meant bad luck
If I had had my wits when heaven's lightning struck
That oak. Still, tell me, Tityrus: who *is* this "god"?

T:

Vrbem quam dicunt Romam, Meliboee, putaui
stultus ego huic nostrae similem, quo saepe solemus 20
pastores ouium teneros depellere fetus.
sic canibus catulos similis, sic matribus haedos
noram, sic paruis componere magna solebam.
uerum haec tantum alias inter caput extulit urbes
quantum lenta solent inter uiburna cupressi. 25

M:

Et quae tanta fuit Romam tibi causa uidendi?

T:

Libertas, quae sera tamen respexit inertem,
candidior postquam tondenti barba cadebat,
respexit tamen et longo post tempore uenit,
postquam nos Amaryllis habet, Galatea reliquit. 30
namque (fatebor enim) dum me Galatea tenebat,
nec spes libertatis erat nec cura peculi.
quamuis multa meis exiret uictima saeptis,
pinguis et ingratae premeretur caseus urbi,
non umquam grauis aere domum mihi dextra redibat. 35

M:

Mirabar quid maesta deos, Amarylli, uocares,
cui pendere sua patereris in arbore poma;
Tityrus hinc aberat. ipsae te, Tityre, pinus,
ipsi te fontes, ipsa haec arbusta uocabant.

T:

Quid facerem? neque seruitio me exire licebat 40

T:

I thought, "Rome must be like our little town." But Rome
Was proof that I was wrong; it's nothing like our home,   20
This place where we would wean the little newborn lambs.
(I learned there pups resemble dogs and kids their dams;
That small forms mimic bigger ones.) Rome's not like those,
However. Rising over every city, she's
A cypress towering above a guelder rose.   25

M:

What made it possible for you to visit Rome?

T:

The goddess Liberty. Though late, she smiled on me—
A slug whose barbered beard was white when it was sheared.
She smiled on me when Galatea finally
Was gone and Amaryllis here. I must confess,   30
While Galatea still possessed me, liberty
Was hopeless, and I couldn't save a blessed thing
Despite the untold victims sold from my sheepfold,
And fat rich cheeses pressed for an ungrateful town.
Not once did I come home with coins that weighed me down.   35

M:

So *that's* why you so sadly begged the deities,
Amaryllis, leaving ripe apples on the trees:
Your Tityrus was gone! And Tityrus, the pines
And springs and orchards all were calling you back home.

T:

What could I do, indentured in my weightless chains?   40

nec tam praesentis alibi cognoscere diuos.
hic illum uidi iuuenem, Meliboee, quotannis,
bis senos cui nostra dies altaria fumant.
hic mihi responsum primus dedit ille petenti:
"pascite ut ante boues, pueri; summittite tauros."   45

M:

Fortunate senex, ergo tua rura manebunt
et tibi magna satis, quamuis lapis omnia nudus
limosoque palus obducat pascua iunco:
non insueta grauis temptabunt pabula fetas,
nec mala uicini pecoris contagia laedent.   50
fortunate senex, hic inter flumina nota
et fontis sacros frigus captabis opacum;
hinc tibi, quae semper, uicino ab limite saepes
Hyblaeis apibus florem depasta salicti
saepe leui somnum suadebit inire susurro;   55
hinc alta sub rupe canet frondator ad auras,
nec tamen interea raucae, tua cura, palumbes
nec gemere aëria cessabit turtur ab ulmo.

T:

Ante leues ergo pascentur in aethere cerui
et freta destituent nudos in litore piscis,   60
ante pererratis amborum finibus exsul
aut Ararim Parthus bibet aut Germania Tigrim,
quam nostro illius labatur pectore uultus.

M:

At nos hinc alii sitientis ibimus Afros,
pars Scythiam et rapidum cretae ueniemus Oaxen   65

And where else could I find such ready gods? For there
I saw him, Meliboeus. Now, throughout the year—
Each month—my altar smokes for that young man, the first
Who listened to my prayer and spoke: "My children, graze
Your cattle as you used to—bulls to breed and raise."   45

M:

Old man, you're lucky, since these acres stay with you—
More than enough, though naked stones pave every patch,
And reeds from muddy marshes make for plastered pastures.
At least no toxic fodder tempts the pregnant ewe;
No neighboring flocks infect your sheep with scab or pox.   50
Old man, you're lucky. Here, amid familiar brooks
And sacred springs, you'll search out cool, refreshing shade.
And near your neighbor's boundary, as it always did,
The hedge that keeps the bees of Hybla willow-fed
Will often lull you to your sleep with soft susurrus.   55
Below the bluff, a pruner tunes the air with airs,
While all along, the doves who are your special care
Coo with the moaning doves in immemorial elms.

T:

The gentle deer will crop the firmament, therefore;
The waves will wash the fish they've stranded on the shore;   60
The vagrant Parthians will drink the Arar, or
The Germans race to drain the Tigris long before
The precious memory of *his* face will be no more.

M:

But *we* must leave here, some for searing Africa,
Some, Scythia or the Oaxes, sluicing Crete.   65

et penitus toto diuisos orbe Britannos.
en umquam patrios longo post tempore finis
pauperis et tuguri congestum caespite culem,
post aliquot, mea regna, uidens mirabor aristas?
impius haec tam culta noualia miles habebit,   70
barbarus has segetes. en quo discordia ciuis
produxit miseros: his nos conseuimus agros!
insere nunc, Meliboee, piros, pone ordine uitis.
ite meae, felix quondam pecus, ite capellae.
non ego uos posthac uiridi proiectus in antro   75
dumosa pendere procul de rupe uidebo;
carmina nulla canam; non me pascente, capellae,
florentem cytisum et salices carpetis amaras.

T:
Hic tamen hanc mecum poteras requiescere noctem
fronde super uiridi; sunt nobis mitia poma,   80
castaneae molles et pressi copia lactis,
et iam summa procul uillarum culmina fumant
maioresque cadunt altis de montibus umbrae.

A scant few, Britain—where all severance is complete.
Long years from now, when I recall my native land—
My poor man's roof piled thick with sod—what will I see?
The realm I called my own when it was eared with wheat?
Will some ungodly soldier claim these plowed-up furrows,   70
Some foreigner these crops? You see where civil war
Has led? These are the sorts of men we planted for.
Go, Meliboeus. Plant your pear trees; set your vines.
My flock once blessed with luck, come on. Come, little ones.
I'll never lie at length again in some green dell   75
To watch you rooted to the distant, leafy bluff.
I'll sing no more, kids; now your grazing days are over;
Your browsing on the bitter willows or the clover.

T:

Well, here's a place to sleep. Come join me; take your rest
On still-green grasses for a bed. I have soft chestnuts,   80
Ripe apples, and a good supply of cheese just pressed.
Already, smoke curls from the highest chimney top,
As from the mountain summits, longer shadows drop.

ECLOGA II

Formosum pastor Corydon ardebat Alexin,
delicias domini, nec quid speraret habebat.
tantum inter densas, umbrosa cacumia, fagos
adsidue ueniebat. ibi haec incondita solus
montibus et siluis studio iactabat inani: 5
"O crudelis Alexi, nihil mea carmina curas?
nil nostri miserere? mori me denique cogis?
nunc etiam pecudes umbras et frigora captant,
nunc uiridis etiam occultant spineta lacertos,
Thestylis et rapido fessis messoribus aestu   10
alia serpyllumque herbas contundit olentis.
at mecum raucis, tua dum uestigia lustro,
sole sub ardenti resonant arbusta cicadis.
nonne fuit satius tristis Amaryllidis iras
atque superba pati fastidia? nonne Menalcan,   15
quamuis ille niger, quamuis tu candidus esses?
o formose puer, nimium ne crede colori:
alba ligustra cadunt, uaccinia nigra leguntur.
despectus tibi sum, nec qui sim quaeris, Alexi,
quam diues pecoris, niuei quam lactis abundans.   20
mille meae Siculis errant in montibus agnae;
lac mihi non aestate nouum, non frigore defit.
canto quae solitus, si quando armenta uocabat,
Amphion Dircaeus in Actaeo Aracyntho.

ECLOGUE II

The shepherd Corydon was burning for Alexis,
His master's fair delight, but had no hope in sight.
Only, he haunted woods so thick with beech their crowns
Made shade, and doggedly he'd sing to hills and trees.
Lonely in love, he threw out artless lines like these: 5
"Heartless Alexis, can't you care about my songs?
No pity, boy? Some day, you'll be the death of me.
Right now, cool shade is being sought by herded throngs;
And even now, green geckoes hide in thorny thickets,
As Thestylis is pestling sweet garlic cloves   10
And thyme for mowers cut down by the scorching heat.
But all alone beneath that sun, as vineyard crickets
Whistle, I track the steps you took with wandering feet.
To suffer Amaryllis' sullen angers and
Her sneering scorn: would that have been far better? Or   15
Menalcas's, though he is dark and you are fair?
But fairest boy, don't count on that fine face too much.
Dark hyacinths get plucked; white flowers die untouched.
Though you look down on me, you don't see what is there,
Alexis: giant herds; white milk jars free of curds;   20
A thousand lambs that range the hills of Sicily;
Fresh snow-white milk that's there in summer and in winter.
I'm like Amphion as he sang, on Aracynthus,
In Attica, to call his herds (he was Dircean).

nec sum adeo informis: nuper me in litore uidi,   25
cum placidum uentis staret mare. non ego Daphnin
iudice te metuam, si numquam fallit imago.
o tantum libeat mecum tibi sordida rura
atque humilis habitare casas et figere ceruos,
haedorumque gregem uiridi compellere hibisco!   30
mecum una in siluis imitabere Pana canendo
(Pan primum calamos cera coniungere pluris
instituit, Pan curat ouis ouiumque magistros),
nec te paeniteat calamo triuisse labellum:
haec eadem ut sciret, quid non faciebat Amyntas?   35
est mihi disparibus septem compacta cicutis
fistula, Damoetas dono mihi quam dedit olim,
et dixit moriens: "te nunc habet ista secundum";
dixit Dameotas, inuidit stultus Amyntas.
praeterea duo nec tuta mihi ualle reperti   40
capreoli, sparsis etiam nunc pellibus albo,
bina die siccant ouis ubera; quos tibi seruo.
iam pridem a me illos abducere Thestylis orat;
et faciet, quoniam sordent tibi munera nostra.
huc ades, o formose puer: tibi lilia plenis   45
ecce ferunt Nymphae calathis; tibi candida Nais,
pallentis uiolas et summa papauera carpens,
narcissum et florem iungit bene olentis anethi;
tum casia atque aliis intexens suauibus herbis
mollia luteola pingit uaccinia calta.   50
ipse ego cana legam tenera lanugine mala
castaneasque nuces, mea quas Amaryllis amabat;
addam cerea pruna (honos erit huic quoque pomo),
et uos, o lauri, carpam et te, proxima myrte,
sic positae quoniam suauis miscetis odores.   55

And I'm not all *that* ugly. By the placid sea   25
Just recently, I saw myself. I wouldn't fear
Daphnis, if *you* were judge . . . if mirrors' truths were clear.
Oh, it would be so good to have you live with me
In just a rustic hut. We'd rough it, shooting deer,
Driving our flocks to graze on green hibiscus. You   30
Could play at Sylvan Pan, and rival him in song
(Pan was the first to teach man how to join the syrinx
With wax. Pan watches over sheep and shepherds, too.)
You'd never rue your reed-worn lip. And when one thinks
Of all the learning pains Amyntas suffered through!   35
I have a panpipe linking seven different lengths
Of hemlock stalk; Damoetas, dying, gave me this
One day, and said, 'It owns *you* now—its second master.'
That's what he said. And then Amyntas envied me—
That dunce. What else? Two kids who've flirted with disaster 40
(I found them in a cleft, their hides still newborn-white).
Daily they drain two udders dry. They're yours, I promise . . .
Though Thestylis has pestered me to have them. (She
May well succeed, since they seem worthless in your sight.)
Come here, O fair, sweet boy. The Nymphs bring lilies—see?—   45
Piled high in wicker baskets. Dazzling Naiads picking
Pale violets and plucking poppy heads are mixing
Narcissus with the fragrant anise. Each one weaves
Mezereon with herbs and aromatic leaves.
Slight hyacinth sets off bright marigold. And me?   50
I'll take up fruit with pale, soft fuzz—the tender quinces—
And chestnuts, which my Amaryllis loved. I'll add
Some waxy plums as well (I won't forget that fruit),
Then cut some laurels and some myrtle sprigs to suit.
When all mixed up, they yield such pleasing fragrances.   55

rusticus es, Corydon; nec munera curat Alexis,
nec, si muneribus certes, concedat Iollas.
heu heu, quid uolui misero mihi? floribus Austrum
perditus et liquidis immisi fontibus apros.
quem fugis, a! demens? habitarunt di quoque siluas   60
Dardaniusque Paris. Pallas quas condidit arces
ipsa colat; nobis placeant ante omnia siluae.
torua leaena lupum sequitur, lupus ipse capellam,
florentem cytisum sequitur lasciua capella,
te Corydon, o Alexi: trahit sua quemque uoluptas.   65
aspice, aratra iugo referunt suspensa iuuenci,
et sol crescentis decedens deplicat umbras;
me tamen urit amor: quis enim modus adsit amori?
a, Corydon, Corydon, quae te dementia cepit!
semiputata tibi frondosa uitis in ulmo est: 70
quin tu aliquid saltem potius, quorum indiget usus,
uiminibus mollique paras detexere iunco?
inuenies alium, se te hic fastidit, Alexin."

Hick Corydon, Alexis doesn't give two pins
For you, and in a giving match, Iollas wins.
So foolishly, I've wished for ... what? I've loosed the blight
Of Auster on my flowers; boars defile my springs.
Demented man, whom are you running from? The gods   60
Once lived in woods—yes, Paris, too. And Pallas? Let her
Keep citadels she built herself; the woods are right
For me. The savage lioness goes hunting, springs
Upon the wolf, the wolf the goat, the goat on buds
Of clover. Corydon, like them, pursues Alexis.   65
So each is drawn by his desire. But look: yoked bulls
Pull back the dangling plough as sunset grows the shadows.
And still I burn with love (yet what can limit love?).
O Corydon, O Corydon! What *is* this madness?
From off the leafy elm, your vine, half trained up, falls.   70
Why not go weave instead some good thing you have need of,
From osier reeds? If this Alexis spurns you, shun
The boy—then go and find yourself another one."

ECLOGA III

Menalcas:

Dic mihi, Damoeta, cuium pecus? an Meliboei?

Damoetas:

Non, uerum Aegonis; nuper mihi tradidit Aegon.

M:

Infelix o semper, oues, pecus! ipse Neaeram
dum fouet ac ne me sibi praeferat illa ueretur,
hic alienus ouis custos bis mulget in hora,   5
et sucus pecori et lac subducitur agnis.

D:

Parcius ista uiris tamen obicienda memento.
nouimus et qui te transuersa tuentibus hircis
et quo (sed faciles Nymphae risere) sacello.

M:

Tum, credo, cum me arbustum uidere Miconis   10
atque mala uitis incidere falce nouellas.

D:

Aut hic ad ueteres fagos cum Daphnidis arcum
fregisti et calamos: quae tu, peruerse Menalca,

ECLOGUE III

Menalcas:

Tell me whose flock, Damoetas. Meliboeus's?

Damoetas:

No, Aegon's, *and* he just entrusted it to me.

M:

Pity the flock, then, since they're clearly out of luck.
He courts Neaera now (afraid that she loves me),
While you—a hired herder—milk the mothers twice   5
An hour, draining the flocks and robbing lambs of suck.

D:

More sparing, please, when charging men with sins like these!
We know whom *you* were with, goats gazing on askance—
And in what shrine, despite the wood Nymphs' lenient glance.

M:

That day they saw me—I suppose—hack Micon's trees   10
And newly growing grapevines with my wicked sickle?

D:

Or here, beside the ancient beeches, when you broke
Both Daphnis' bow and arrows, since you grew perverse,

et cum uidisti puero donata, dolebas,
et si non aliqua nocuisses, mortuus esses.   15

M:

Quid domini faciant, audent cum talia fures?
non ego te uidi Damonis, pessime, caprum
excipere insidiis multum latrante Lycisca?
et cum clamarem "quo nunc se proripit ille?
Tityre, coge pecus," tu post carecta latebas.   20

D:

An mihi cantando uictius non redderet ille,
quem mea carminibus meruisset fistula caprum?
si nescis, meus ille caper fuit; et mihi Damon
ipse fatebatur, sed reddere posse negabat.

M:

Cantando tu illum? aut umquam tibi fistula cera   25
iuncta fuit? non tu in triuiis, indocte, solebas
stridenti miserum stipula disperdere carmen?

D:

Vis ergo inter nos quid possit uterque uicissim
experiamur? ego hanc uitulam (ne forte recuses,
bis uenit ad mulctram, binos alit ubere fetus)   30
depono; tu dic mecum quo pignore certes.

M:

De grege non ausim quicquam deponere tecum:
est mihi namque domi pater, est iniusta nouerca,
bisque die numerant ambo pecus, alter et haedos.

Menalcas—full of spite—when he first got those gifts.
And if you hadn't done him wrong, you would have choked.   15

M:

What can the masters do when lowlifes grow so daring?
Didn't I see you, wretch, lying in wait for snaring
That goat from Damon, even though Lycisca barked?
And when I cried out, "Where's *he* running? Watch your flock,
Tityrus!" you went ducking down behind the sedges.   20

D:

But was he going to give me what my song had won—
The goat my piper's tunes deserved? You may not know it,
But Damon had admitted that I'd won that goat,
Though paying me was something that "could not be done."

M:

You outplayed *him?* Well, do you now, or did you once,   25
Possess a wax-joined pipe? Confess: you were that dunce
At crossroads, killing wretched songs on scrannel pipes.

D:

That *does* it! Care to test what each of us can do
In turn? I'll stake this heifer here, so don't back out.
Milked twice a day, she still can suckle two new calves.   30
What will you bet? And don't be wagering by halves!

M:

I can't bet something from the herd—not on my life.
(At home's a father ... and his wicked second wife.
Both count the flocks twice, *and* she counts the kids as well).

uerum, id quod multo tute ipse fatebere maius   35
(insanire libet quoniam tibi), pocula ponam
fagina, caelatum diuini opus Alcimedontis,
lenta quibus torno facili superaddita uitis
diffusos hedera uestit pallente corymbos.
in medio duo signa, Conon et—quis fuit alter,   40
descripsit radio totum qui gentibus orbem,
tempora quae messor, quae curuus arator haberet?
necdum illis labra admoui, sed condita seruo.

D:

Et nobis idem Alcimedon duo pocula fecit
et molli circum est ansas amplexus acantho,   45
Orpheaque in medio posuit siluasque sequentis;
necdum illis labra admoui, sed condita seruo.
si ad uitulam spectas, nihil est quod pocula laudes.

M:

Numquam hodie effugies; ueniam quocumque uocaris.
audiat haec tantum—uel qui uenit ecce Palaemon.   50
efficiam posthac ne quemquam uoce lacessas.

D:

Quin age, si quid habes; in me mora non erit ulla,
nec quemquam fugio; tantum, uicine Palaemon,
sensibus haec imis (res est non parua) reponas.

Palaemon:

Dicite, quandoquidem in molli consedimus herba.   55
et nunc omnis ager, nunc omnis parturit arbos,
nunc frondent siluae, nunc formosissimus annus.

But since you will admit yourself they're worth far more,   35
And since you're mad enough, I'll bet these beechwood cups—
Alcimedon's supernal carving craftsmanship.
His fluent knife has given them a supple vine;
Through berries bunched on pale green ivy, see it twine.
Two figures dominate: there's Conon and—who *else*,   40
Whose rod surveyed the universe for humankind,
And told men when to plow, and when to reap and bind?
My lips have not yet sipped these cups; I've set them by.

D:

Alcimedon has made two cups for me, as well,
And banding soft acanthus leaves about the handles,   45
Has centered Orpheus, with trees drawn by his spell.
My lips have not yet sipped these cups; I've set them by.
But see my heifer, and you'll never praise my cups.

M:

You cannot stall me now, no matter where you call me.
But there should be a judge . . . and look! Palaemon's coming.   50
I'll see you never challenge any singer . . . ever!

D:

Come on, then, if you can. You won't see *me* back down;
No referee can frighten *me*. But friend Palaemon:
Focus, and do your best; this is no time to clown.

Palaemon:

Well, since we're on this soft green grass, begin to sing.   55
Each pasture, every tree, begins its burgeoning.
Now woods are in full leaf; the year is at its best.

incipe, Damoeta; tu deinde sequere Menalca.
alternis dicetis; amant alterna Camenae.

D:

Ab Ioue principium, Musae: Iouis omnia plena;   60
ille colit terras, illi mea carmina curae.

M:

Et me Phoebus amat; Phoebo sua semper apud me
munera sunt, lauri et suaue rubens hyacinthus.

D:

Malo me Galatea petit, lasciua puella,
et fugit ad salices et se cupit ante uideri.   65

M:

At mihi sese offert ultro, meus ignis, Amyntas,
notior ut iam sit canibus non Delia nostris.

D:

Parta meae Veneri sunt munera: namque notaui
ipse locum, aëriae quo congessere palumbes.

M:

Quod potui, puero siluestri ex arbore lecta   70
aurea mala decem misi; cras altera mittam.

D:

O quotiens et quae nobis Galatea locuta est!
partem aliquam, uenti, diuum referatis ad auris!

Begin, Damoetas. Then, Menalcas, follow, singing
In turn. Such alternation gratifies the Muses.

D:

Great Sisters, Jove is where I start, whose force infuses   60
Everything. He blesses earth; he tends my songs.

M:

Phoebus loves me; to him my every gift belongs—
Both laurel and the hyacinth that blushes flame.

D:

Loose Galatea apples me (yes, that's her aim);
Down by the sally gardens, then, she hopes for capture.   65

M:

He gives himself unasked—Amyntas, who's my rapture.
My pooches know him better than the moonlit skies.

D:

My Venus loves the gifts I give; with my own eyes
I've seen where wood-doves build their high and airy nest.

M:

From tree limbs in the woods, I sent my very best—   70
Ten golden apples. Soon, I'll send my love ten more.

D:

The *things* that Galatea's said! Who could keep score?
So heaven's ears may hear: winds, waft just some of them.

M:

Quid prodest, quod me ipse animo non spernis, Amynta,
si, dum tu sectaris apros, ego retia seruo?   75

D:

Phyllida mitte mihi: meus est natalis, Iolla;
cum faciam uitula pro frugibus, ipse uenito.

M:

Phyllida amo ante alias; nam me discedere fleuit
et longum "formose, uale, uale," inquit, "Iolla."

D:

Triste lupus stabulis, maturis frugibus imbres,   80
arboribus uenti, nobis Amaryllidis irae.

M:

Dulce satis umor, depulsis arbutus haedis,
lenta salix feto pecori, mihi solus Amyntas.

D:

Pollio amat nostram, quamuis est rustica, Musam:
Pierides uitulam lectori pascite uestro.   85

M:

Pollio et ipse facit noua carmina: pascite taurum,
iam cornu petat et pedibus qui spargat harenam.

D:

Qui te, Pollio, amat, ueniat quo te quoque gaudet;
mella fluant illi, ferat et rubus asper amomum.

M:

Amyntas, I've a heart you say you won't contemn,
But then you hunt the boar and leave me mending nets.   75

D:

Iollas, send me Phyllis for my birthday fêtes;
When I have killed a harvest heifer, you come, too.

M:

It's Phyllis I love best; she wept at my adieu,
Crying at length, "Farewell, Iollas fair; farewell."

D:

Cruel is *lupus*, raider of pens; to crops, the hale   80
Is fell, to trees the gales; to me, my Amaryllis.

M:

Sweet is the rain to seeds; to new-weaned kids, arbutus;
To flocks, soft willow. Amaryllis is to me.

D:

Pollio loves my Muse, bucolic though she be.
Pierides, your readers need a calf fed full.   85

M:

Pollio sings new songs himself; fatten a bull
That flaunts his horns, then hooves the sand and makes it fly.

D:

Pollio, may friends be glad where you are (there, nearby!);
May honey flow, and spice be what the bramble bears.

M:

Qui Bauium non odit, amet tua carmina, Maeui,   90
atque idem iungat uulpes et mulgeat hircos.

D:

Qui legitis flores et humi nascentia fraga,
frigidus, o pueri (fugite hinc!), latet anguis in herba.

M:

Parcite, oues, nimium procedere: non bene ripae
creditur; ipse aries etiam nunc uellera siccat.   95

D:

Tityre, pascentis a flumine reice capellas:
ipse, ubi tempus erit, omnis in fonte lauabo.

M:

Cogite ouis, pueri: si lac praeceperit aestus,
ut nuper, frustra pressabimus ubera palmis.

D:

Heu heu, quam pingui macer est mihi taurus in eruo!   100
idem amor exitium est pecori pecorisque magistro.

M:

His certe neque amor causa est; uix ossibus haerent;
nescio quis teneros oculus mihi fascinat agnos.

D:

Dic quibus in terris (et eris mihi magnus Apollo)
tris pateat caeli spatium non amplius ulnas.   105

M:

Let Bavius' admirers love Maevius' airs ...   90
And yoke a pair of foxes ... after milking billies.

D:

Children who search the ground for berries and for lilies,
Run! Run away! Low in the grass, a cool snake hides.

M:

Don't go too far, my sheep, or trust the riversides
Too much. Right now, the ram dries out his fleece. Just look.   95

D:

Tityrus, turn the grazing goats back from the brook;
When it comes time for that, I'll give the sheep their dip.

M:

Boys, herd the ewes. If udders shrivel to a drip—
This heat of late—our palms will grip their teats in vain.

D:

Gaunt in the fattening vetch, my pining bull's in pain.   100
This love will ruin both the herdsman and the herd.

M:

They're skin and bones; that love would cause this is absurd.
My tender lambs are hexed, but by whose evil eye?

D:

You'd be my great Apollo? Tell me where the sky
Extends no wider than three times a human ell.   105

M:

Dic quibus in terris inscripti nomina regum
nascantur flores, et Phyllida solus habeto.

P:

Non nostrum inter uos tantas componere lites:
et uitula tu dignus et hic, et quisquis amores
aut metuet dulcis aut experietur amaros.   110
claudite iam riuos, pueri; sat prata biberunt.

M:

And *you'll* have Phyllis to yourself if you can tell
Where flowers bloom with royal names scribed on their petals.

P:

It's not for me to say who's shown the heartiest mettle.
You've earned the heifer both—and any one who trembles
Testing the sweeter love, or tasting love that's bitter.   110
The fields have had their fill, boys; close the sluices' shutters.

Sicelides Musae, paulo maiora canamus!
non omnis arbusta iuuant humilesque myricae;
si canimus siluas, siluae sint consule dignae.
    Vltima Cumaei uenit iam carminis aetas;
magnus ab integro saeclorum nascitur ordo.   5
iam redit et Virgo, redeunt Saturnia regna,
iam noua progenies caelo demittitur alto.
tu modo nascenti puero, quo ferrea primum
desinet ac toto surget gens aurea mundo,
casta faue Lucina: tuus iam regnat Apollo.   10
teque adeo decus hoc aeui, te consule, inibit,
Pollio, et incipient magni procedere menses;
te duce, si qua manent sceleris uestigia nostri,
inrita perpetua soluent formidine terras.
ille deum uitam accipiet diuisque uidebit   15
permixtos heroas et ipse uidebitur illis,
pacatumque reget patriis uirtutibus orbem.
    At tibi prima, puer, nullo munuscula cultu
errantis hederas passim cum baccare tellus
mixtaque ridenti colocasia fundet acantho.   20
ipsae lacte domum referent distenta capellae
ubera, nec magnos metuent armenta leones;
ipsa tibi blandos fundent cunabula flores.
occidet et serpens, et fallax herba ueneni

ECLOGUE IV

Sicilian Muses, let my theme be somewhat greater.
Forests are not for all, nor lowly tamarisks.
(But if I sing woods, make them worthy of a leader.)
The final age of Cumae's prophecies has come,
Now the great long line of the ages is begun.   5
The Virgin now returns, and Saturn's golden regnum.
Now come new generations down on high from heaven.
O chaste Lucina, you need only bless this boy
Just born and then the Iron Age will end. A *gens*
Of gold will fill the globe. Now, your Apollo reigns.   10
Yes, Pollio: in your consulship this age of joy
And glory, as the great months start their march, begins.
Leading us, you'll erase all traces of our sins
Remaining, freeing earth from endless fear and strife.
Seeing the gods, *he'll* join in their celestial life.   15
Where gods and heroes mingle, he'll be seen among them,
Ruling a world his father's virtues blessed with peace.
But newborn boy, for you, these presents shall pour forth—
Cyclamen first, with ivy spread all over earth,
Then colocasia mixed in with acanthus smiling.   20
All by themselves, the goats shall bring milk-swollen udders
Home, and herds faced with mighty lions shall not shudder.
All on its own, your cradle will provide you blossoms.
Death, even for the snake; and for all poison plants,

occidet; Assyrium uulgo nascetur amomum.   25
at simul heroum laudes et facta parentis
iam legere et quae sit poteris cognoscere uirtus,
molli paulatim flauescet campus arista
incultisque rubens pendebit sentibus uua
et durae quercus sudabunt roscida mella.   30
pauca tamen suberunt priscae uestigia fraudis,
quae temptare Thetim ratibus, quae cingere muris
oppida, quae iubeant telluri infindere sulcos.
alter erit tum Tiphys et altera quae uehat Argo
delectos heroas; erunt etiam altera bella   35
atque iterum ad Troiam magnus mittetur Achilles.
hinc, ubi iam firmata uirum te fecerit aetas,
cedet et ipse mari uector, nec nautica pinus
mutabit merces; omnis feret omnia tellus.
non rastros patietur humus, non uinea falcem;   40
robustus quoque iam tauris iuga soluet arator.
nec uarios discet mentiri lana colores,
ipse sed in pratis aries iam suaue rubenti
murice, iam croceo mutabit uellera luto;
sponte sua sandyx pascentis uestiet agnos.   45
     "Talia saecla" suis dixerunt "currite" fusis
concordes stabili fatorum numine Parcae.
adgredere o magnos (aderit iam tempus) honores,
cara deum suboles, magnum Iouis incrementum!
aspice conuexo nutantem pondere mundum,   50
terrasque tractusque maris caelumque profundum;
aspice, uenturo laetentur ut omnia saeclo!
o mihi tum longae maneat pars ultima uitae,
spiritus et quantum sat erit tua dicere facta!
non me carminibus uincet nec Thracius Orpheus   55

Death, too. Assyrian amomum will grow common.   25
As soon as you can read of heroes and the deeds
Your father's done, and learn what manly valor means,
Then, gradually, the grain shall grow in golden fields,
While purpling grapes depend from brakes with thorns gone wild,
And hard, enduring oaks sweat dewy honey. Yet man's   30
First tragic error and its fruits shall linger, prompting
His ships to challenge Thetis. Walls will cinch the girths
Of towns, and plows inflict their furrows on the earth.
There'll be another Tiphys and another *Argo*
Carrying off to war its prime, heroic cargo,   35
As one more great Achilles goes to Troy to war.
Later, when strength of years has made a man of you,
The sailing merchants and their pine-built ships will stop.
There'll be no trading goods; all lands will bear all crops.
The soil will never suffer hoe, nor vine the hook.   40
Then sturdy plowmen will unyoke their bulls. Our wool
Will fabricate the lies of varied dyes no more;
Pied coats of many colors will be worn by rams—
Now raddled murex, now a saffron yellow fleece.
Spontaneous scarlet will redress the peaceful lambs.   45
"May times like these run on," the Fates sang to their spindles,
Concordant with the ordered will of Destiny.
Oh, enter on your coming glory; time draws near,
Great child of Jove and heir to gods who hold you dear!
The landed world's great round bows down, its huge head bent; 50
So do the sea and the eternal firmament.
See how they all rejoice at time's new age to come!
Oh, may I still have some last part of life this long—
Just breath enough—to celebrate your myriad deeds!
Not Thracian Orpheus nor Linus, with a mother's   55

nec Linus, huic mater quamuis atque huic pater adsit,
Orphei Calliopea, Lino formosus Apollo,
Pan etiam, Arcadia mecum si iudice certet,
Pan etiam Arcadia dicat se iudice uictum.

    Incipe, parue puer, risu cognoscere matrem   60
(matri longa decem tulerunt fastidia menses)
incipe, parue puer: qui non risere parenti,
nec deus hunc mensa, dea nec dignata cubili est.

Or father's aid, would better me in any song.
(Calliope her Orpheus; Apollo, Linus).
Even if Pan should try me with Arcadia judging,
Pan still would say, Arcadia judging, that he'd lost.
Begin, boy infant: smile—to show you know your mother.   60
Ten lengthy months have meant much patience, pain, and bother.
Begin, boy infant. Goddesses will bed no child—
Nor gods board one—on whom his parents have not smiled.

Menalcas:

Cur non, Mopse, boni quoniam conuenimus ambo,
tu calamos inflare leuis, ego dicere uersus,
hic corylis mixtas inter consedimus ulmos?

Mopsus:

Tu maior; tibi me est aequum parere, Menalca,
siue sub incertas Zephyris motantibus umbras   5
siue antro potius succedimus. aspice, ut antrum
siluestris raris sparsit labrusca racemis.

Me:

Montibus in nostris solus tibi certat Amyntas.

Mo:

Quid, si idem certet Phoebum superare canendo?

Me:

Incipe, Mopse, prior, si quos aut Phyllidis ignis   10
aut Alconis habes laudes aut iurgia Codri.
incipe: pascentis seruabit Tityrus haedos.

Mo:

Immo haec, in uiridi nuper quae cortice fagi

ECLOGUE V

Menalcas:

Well, Mopsus, here we are—a pair of talents (one
For singing to the pipe and one for playing it).
With elms and scattered hazels all around, let's sit.

Mopsus:

Menalcas, you're my senior, so it's only right
I go along if you would like to find a cave—   5
Or shade the Zephyr shakes. See how the wild vine makes
Its clusters wreathe the cave mouth like an architrave.

Me:

Amyntas is your only rival in these parts.

Mo:

As if *his* singing put to shame Apollo's art!

Me:

Mopsus, begin with any song—the loves of Phyllis,   10
Or Alcon's praises, or some raillery at Codrus.
Begin, and Tityrus will tend the grazing kids.

Mo:

No, no. Instead, I'll try this song just carved on green

carmina descripsi et modulans alterna notaui,
experiar: tu deinde iubeto ut certet Amyntas.   15

Me:

Lenta salix quantum pallenti cedit oliuae,
puniceis humilis quantum saliunca rosetis,
iudicio nostro tantum tibi cedit Amyntas.
sed tu desine plura, puer: successimus antro.

Mo:

Exstinctum Nymphae crudeli funere Daphnin   20
flebant (uos coryli testes et flumina Nymphis),
cum complexa sui corpus miserabile nati
atque deos atque astra uocat crudelia mater.
non ulli pastos illis egere diebus
frigida, Daphni, boues ad flumina; nulla neque amnem   25
libauit quadripes nec graminis attigit herbam.
Daphni, tuum Poenos etiam ingemuisse leones
interitum montesque feri siluaeque loquuntur.
Daphnis et Armenias curru subiungere tigris
instituit, Daphnis thiasos inducere Bacchi   30
et foliis lentas intexere mollibus hastas.
uitis ut arboribus decori est, ut uitibus uuae,
ut gregibus tauri, segetes ut pinguibus aruis,
tu decus omne tuis. postquam te fata tulerunt,
ipsa Pales agros atque ipse reliquit Apollo.   35
grandia saepe quibus mandauimus hordea sulcis,
infelix lolium et steriles nascuntur auenae;
pro molli uiola, pro purpureo narcisso
carduus et spinis surgit paliurus acutis.
spargite humum foliis, inducite fontibus umbras,   40

Beech bark, the words and tune set down in turn. Then if
You like, command Amyntas' pipe to challenge mine.   15

Me:

Before the pale grey olive tree, the willow bows;
The pink valerian acknowledges the rose.
That's how I think Amyntas bows to you in song.
But here's the cave, son; we've been talking far too long.

Mo:

"You streams and hazel trees: the cruel death Daphnis died,   20
Now testify to (how the grieving Nymphs all cried).
Cradling the body of the son who once was hers,
His mother called them savage both—the gods and stars.
And Daphnis, in those days, no drover led the grazing
Cattle to cooling brooks. Not one four-footed creature   25
Would quench his thirst; not one partook of grass at pasture.
Daphnis, the wildest woods and highest hills still tell us
That even Punic lions groaned at what befell you.
Daphnis first taught men how to yoke Armenian tigers
To chariots. Daphnis first led the Bacchic chorus;   30
Because of him, around our spears the vine entwines.
As vine leaves honor trees, and grapes in bunches, vines;
As bullock graces herd, and grain the fertile field:
So, Daphnis, you to all the folk. Since you were borne
Away by Fate, both Pales and Apollo scorn   35
Our land. Too often, furrows sown with good big barley
Have raised up sterile stalks of oats and wretched darnel.
We look for silken violet and blush narcissus,
But get the spiked and bristling thorn and growing thistle.
Shepherds, spread petals on the ground; drape springs in shade.   40

pastores (mandat fieri sibi talia Daphnis),
et tumulum facite, et tumulo superaddite carmen:
"Daphnis ego in siluis, hinc usque ad sidera notus,
formosi pecoris custos, formosior ipse."

Me:

Tale tuum carmen nobis, diuine poeta,   45
quale sopor fessis in gramine, quale per aestum
dulcis aquae saliente sitim restinguere riuo.
nec calamis solum aequiperas, sed uoce magistrum:
fortunate puer, tu nunc eris alter ab illo.
nos tamen haec quocumque modo tibi nostra uicissim   50
dicemus, Daphninque tuum tollemus ad astra;
Daphnin ad astra feremus: amauit nos quoque Daphnis.

Mo:

An quicquam nobis tali sit munere maius?
et puer ipse fuit cantari dignus, et ista
iam pridem Stimichon laudauit carmina nobis.   55

Me:

Candidus insuetum miratur limen Olympi
sub pedibusque uidet nubes et sidera Daphnis.
ergo alacris siluas et cetera rura uoluptas
Panaque pastoresque tenet Dryadasque puellas.
nec lupus insidias pecori, nec retia ceruis   60
ulla dolum meditantur: amat bonus otia Daphnis.
ipsi laetitia uoces ad sidera iactant
intonsi montes; ipsae iam carmina rupes,
ipsa sonant arbusta: "deus, deus ille, Menalca!"
sis bonus o felixque tuis! en quattuor aras: 65

For Daphnis wishes things like these for accolades.
Now build a tomb, and on it, let this verse be made:
I'm woodland Daphnis, known from here to heaven's sill.
Guardian of the finest flock, I'm finer still."

Me:

Celestial poet, when you sing, I think it's like   45
A nap on grass to one who's weary and would slake
His thirst with water from a bubbling summer stream.
Not only with your pipe, but with your voice you match
Your master, and your skill and his are much the same.
Still, hear me sing, in turn, my song—with middling skill.   50
I'll sing your Daphnis to the stars, for good or ill.
Daphnis I'll bear to heaven; he loved me as well.

Mo:

For me, what greater gift than this? Not only was
That boy deserving of a paean, but Stimichon
Was singing me your singing's praise some time ago.   55

Me:

Numinous Daphnis dazzles at the strange new sill
Of heaven, where he sees the clouds and stars below—
The reason why the shepherd's fields and forests fill
With Pan's delight, and with the charming Dryads', too.
Wolves plan no raids on lambs; nets mean no harm to deer.   60
For gentle Daphnis always favors peace. Rejoicing,
The unshorn hills sing out, casting their happy voices
Star-ward, as every rock face echoes with the song
(The copses, too): "He is a god. A god, Menalcas."
Be kind and bless your people. Look at these four altars: 65

ecce duas tibi, Daphni, duas altaria Phoebo.
pocula bina nouo spumantia lacte quotannis
craterasque duo statuam tibi pinguis oliui,
et multo in primis hilarans conuiuia Baccho
(ante focum, si frigus erit; si messis, in umbra)   70
uina nouum fundam calathis Ariusia nectar.
cantabunt mihi Damoetas et Lyctius Aegon;
saltantis Satyros imitabitur Alphesiboeus.
haec tibi semper erunt, et cum sollemnia uota
reddemus Nymphis, et cum lustrabimus agros.   75
dum iuga montis aper, fluuios dum piscis amabit,
dumque thymo pascentur apes, dum rore cicadae,
semper honos nomenque tuum laudesque manebunt.
ut Baccho Cererique, tibi sic uota quotannis
agricolae facient: damnabis tu quoque uotis.   80

Mo:

Quae tibi, quae tali reddam pro carmine dona?
nam neque me tantum uenientis sibilus Austri
nec percussa iuuant fluctu tam litora, nec quae
saxosas inter decurrunt flumina uallis.

Me:

Hac te nos fragili donabimus ante cicuta;   85
haec nos "formosum Corydon ardebat Alexin,"
haec eadem docuit "cuium pecus? an Meliboei?"

Mo:

At tu sume pedum, quod, me cum saepe rogaret,
non tulit Antigenes (et erat tum dignus amari),
formosum paribus nodis atque aere, Menalca.   90

See? Two high stones for Phoebus and for Daphnis, two.
Each year, I'll set two brimming cups of foaming milk,
And two bowls full of rich, fat olive oil, for you.
My prime task (cheering up the banquet with Lord Bacchus)
Means pouring cups of new-wine nectar—Ariusian   70
In winter at the hearth, at harvest in the shade.
Both Aegon and Damoetas shall sing serenades,
Alphesiboeus miming dancing Satyrs.
Your rites shall never end—when we have made the Nymphs
Our solemn vows, and purified the plowman's land.   75
So long as boars love mountain heights, and fish love streams;
So long as crickets drink the dew and bees take thyme;
Your praises shall endure; your honor and your name.
As farmers vow to Ceres, Bacchus, every year,
So you will bind them to their sacred vows as well."   80

Mo:

What gifts can I bestow on you for such a song?
For me, the sibilance of Auster when he comes,
Or waves that pummel summer sands like drums, can't please
As much—nor rivers rushing down their rocky valleys.

Me:

First, here's my gift: the fragile hemlock pipe that taught   85
"The shepherd Corydon was burning for Alexis"
And "Say whose flock, Damoetas. Meliboeus's?"

Mo:

Then take this crook Antigenes has begged from us,
But failed to get (though worthy of this love of mine,
Menalcas). Matching knob and brass make it quite fine.   90

Prima Syracosio dignata est ludere uersu
nostra neque erubuit siluas habitare Thalea.
cum canerem reges et proelia, Cynthius aurem
uellit et admonuit: "pastorem, Tityre, pinguis
pascere oportet ouis, deductum dicere carmen."   5
nunc ego (namque super tibi erunt qui dicere laudes,
Vare, tuas cupiant et tristia condere bella)
agrestem tenui meditabor harundine Musam:
non iniussa cano. si quis tamen haec quoque, si quis
captus amore leget, te nostrae, Vare, myricae,   10
te nemus omne canet; nec Phoebo gratior ulla est
quam sibi quae Vari praescripsit pagina nomen.
    Pergite, Pierides. Chromis et Mnasyllos in antro
Silenum pueri somno uidere iacentem,
inflatum hesterno uenas, ut semper, Iaccho;   15
serta procul tantum capiti delapsa iacebant
et grauis attrita pendebat cantharus ansa.
adgressi (nam saepe senex spe carminis ambo
luserat) iniciunt ipsis ex uincula sertis.
addit se sociam timidisque superuenit Aegle,   20
Aegle Naiadum pulcherrima, iamque uidenti
sanguineis frontem moris et tempora pingit.
ille dolum ridens "quo uincula nectitis?" inquit;
"soluite me, pueri; satis est potuisse uideri.

She never blushed at woodland living—not my Muse—
For Thalia first approved of verse from Syracuse.
But when I sang of royal broils, the Cynthian tugged
My ear and counseled: "Tityrus, a shepherd ought
To feed sheep fat, but sing a song that's spun out thin."   5
Varus, there'll always be a superfluity
Singing your praises, writing frightening martial lays.
So I will court the country Muse on slender reed,
Singing as ordered. But if anyone should heed
These lines, and captivated, love them, all our groves   10
And tamarisks will sing you, Varus. Phoebus loves
That page the best that bears your name inscribed before it.
Proceed, Pierides. The two boys Chromis and
Mnasyllos saw Silenus sleeping in a cave,
Veins thick, as always, from "Iacchus" yesterday.   15
Where it had fallen from his head: a wreath of fronds.
And from a well-worn handle hung his heavy tankard.
Falling upon that codger who'd so often conned
Them of a song they'd longed to hear, they made his very
Garlands bind him. Then Aegle finds them, joins their wary   20
Company (Aegle—charming Naiad). With his eyes
Wide open now, she paints his brow with blood-red berries.
Laughing at such a trick, he asks, "Why binding ties,
Boys? Set me loose. To show what you could do's enough.

carmina quae uultis cognoscite; carmina uobis,   25
huic aliud mercedis erit." simul incipit ipse.
tum uero in numerum Faunosque ferasque uideres
ludere, tum rigidas motare cacumina quercus;
nec tantum Phoebo gaudet Parnasia rupes,
nec tantum Rhodope miratur et Ismarus Orphea.   30
    Namque canebat uti magnum per inane coacta
semina terrarumque animaeque marisque fuissent
et liquidi simul ignis; ut his ex omnia primis,
omnia et ipse tener mundi concreuerit orbis;
tum durare solum et discludere Nerea ponto   35
coeperit et rerum paulatim sumere formas;
iamque nouum terrae stupeant lucescere solem,
altius atque cadant summotis nubibus imbres,
incipiant siluae cum primum surgere cumque
rara per ignaros errent animalia montis.   40
hinc lapides Pyrrhae iactos, Saturnia regna,
Caucasiasque refert uolucris furtumque Promethei.
his adiungit, Hylan nautae quo fonte relictum
clamassent, ut litus "Hyla, Hyla" omne sonaret;
et fortunatam, si numquam armenta fuissent,   45
Pasiphaen niuei solatur amore iuuenci.
a, uirgo infelix, quae te dementia cepit!
Proetides implerunt falsis mugitibus agros,
at non tam turpis pecudum tamen ulla secuta
concubitus, quamuis collo timuisset aratrum   50
et saepe in leui quaesisset cornua fronte.
a! uirgo infelix, tu nunc in montibus erras:
ille latus niueum molli fultus hyacintho
ilice sub nigra pallentis ruminat herbas
aut aliquam in magno sequitur grege. "claudite, Nymphae,   55

Now note the songs you craved. You'll have those songs, while *she*   25
Shall have some other prize." He sang then, and you'd see
The Fauns and feral creatures frisking to his measures,
And all the while, the crowns of stout oaks, bowing, swaying.
Phoebus can't give Parnassus' cliffs such joy, nor Orpheus
Kindle such awe in Rhodope or Ismarus.   30
He sang how through the vastnesses of space the seeds
Of earth and air and seas were fused fast all together
With molten fire; how each new thing and every weather
(Yes, all—even the world's new globe) grew out of these;
How land then started hardening and shut the seas   35
On Nereus, and slowly took its final form;
How dazzled earth beheld both brand new sun at dawn,
And, falling from those built-up cloud heights, rain and storm;
How forests first began to grow; how all uncommon
Creatures would range the mountains that could not yet know them. 40
He tells of Saturn's reign; of Pyrrha's casting stones;
The Caucasus's birds; of that Promethean theft;
And of the spring where Hylas' crew had cried (they'd left
Him lost, their Hylas) till the shore rang "Hylas! Hylas!"
He solaces Pasiphaë—far better off   45
If herds had never been—who loved a snow-white bull.
What madness took possession of you, wretched girl?
(True, Proetus' daughters filled the fields with spurious lowings.
But not one gave in to a furious lust so vile
[For beasts!], although she'd feared her neck might wear a yoke,   50
And felt her downy brow for horns there all the while.)
Poor wretched girl! You roam the mountainsides, while he,
His snow-white flanks supported by soft hyacinth,
Chews the pale grass beneath a dark-boled ilex tree,
Or tracks some great herd's heifer. "Nymphs, close up the glens;   55

Dictaeae Nymphae, nemorum iam claudite saltus,
si qua forte ferant oculis sese obuia nostris
errabunda bouis uestigia; forsitan illum
aut herba captum uiridi aut armenta secutum
perducant aliquae stabula ad Gortynia uaccae." 60
tum canit Hesperidum miratam mala puellam;
tum Phaethontiades musco circumdat amarae
corticis atque solo proceras erigit alnos.
tum canit, errantem Permessi ad flumina Gallum
Aonas in montis ut duxerit una sororum, 65
utque uiro Phoebi chorus adsurrexerit omnis;
ut Linus haec illi, diuino carmine pastor
floribus atque apio crinis ornatus amaro
dixerit: "hos tibi dant calamos (en accipe) Musae,
Ascraeo quos ante seni, quibus ille solebat 70
cantando rigidas deducere montibus ornos.
his tibi Grynei nemoris dicatur origo,
ne quis sit lucus quo se plus iactet Apollo."
   Quid loquar aut Scyllam Nisi, quam fama secuta est
candida succinctam latrantibus inguina monstris 75
Dulichias uexasse rates et gurgite in alto
a! timidos nautas canibus lacerasse marinis;
aut ut mutatos Terei narrauerit artus,
quas illi Philomela dapes, quae dona pararit,
quo cursu deserta petiuerit, et quibus ante 80
infelix sua tecta super uolitauerit alis?
omnia, quae Phoebo quondam meditante, beatus
audiit Eurotas iussitque ediscere lauros,
ille canit, pulsae referunt ad sidera ualles;
cogere donec ouis stabulis numerumque referre 85
iussit et inuito processit Vesper Olympo.

Close them, Dictean Nymphs, if there is any chance
That wandering bull might one day show our eyes his hoofprints,
Here right before us. It might even be, perhaps,
That lured by fresh green fodder, or the herd, he'll trail
Some cow, and find that he's arrived at Gortyn's stalls."   60
He sings of her whom Hesperidean apples stunned,
Then binds, in bitter moss, the sibs of Phaëthon,
Turning them (all his sisters) into long tall alders.
He sings of Gallus by the waters of Permessus,
And how a Sister led him to Aonian heights,   65
Where in his honor rose the whole of Phoebus' chorus.
(Linus, the famous shepherd of celestial song,
His tresses dressed in flowers and in bitter parsley,
Said, "Take these pipe reeds; here—the Muses give what long
Ago they gave the great Ascrean bard, whose song   70
Could tractor stubborn mountain ash down from the slopes.
Use these to say how the Grynean grove began,
That no grove may please Phoebus more than this one can.")
Why speak of Nisus' Scylla, who, the story goes,
Wore howling monsters round her pale white waist, tormented   75
Dulichian ships, deep-sixed them in her maelstrom's throes,
And terrified those mariners with snarling hounds?
Why tell of how he told of Tereus' limbs transformed,
And of the gift of Philomel's cooked offerings;
What course she flew to reach the wasteland, and what wings   80
That poor bird beat to hover over her own roof?
He sang of all that Phoebus dwelled on, ages past
(Which blessed Eurotas heard . . . and ordered that his laurels
Learn). And the pulsing vales re-told it to the stars,
Until Olympian skies saw unsought Vesper come—   85
A sign to pen the flocks and add their twilight sum.

Meliboeus:

Forte sub arguta consederat ilice Daphnis,
compulerantque greges Corydon et Thyrsis in unum,
Thyrsis ouis, Corydon distentas lacte capellas,
ambo florentes aetatibus, Arcades ambo,
et cantare pares et respondere parati.   5
huc mihi, dum teneras defendo a frigore myrtos,
uir gregis ipse caper deerrauerat; atque ego Daphnin
aspicio. ille ubi me contra uidet, "ocius" inquit
"huc ades, O Meliboee; caper tibi saluus et haedi;
et, si quid cessare potes, requiesce sub umbra.   10
huc ipsi potum uenient per prata iuuenci,
hic uiridis tenera praetexit harundine ripas
Mincius, eque sacra resonant examina quercu."
quid facerem? neque ego Alcippen nec Phyllida habebam
depulsos a lacte domi quae clauderet agnos,   15
et certamen erat, Corydon cum Thyrside, magnum;
posthabui tamen illorum mea seria ludo.
alternis igitur contendere uersibus ambo
coepere, alternos Musae meminisse uolebant.
hos Corydon, illos referebat in ordine Thyrsis.   20

Corydon:

Nymphae noster amor Libethrides, aut mihi carmen,

ECLOGUE VII

Meliboeus:

It happened Daphnis sat beneath a singing ilex.
Thyrsis and Corydon had drawn up both their flocks—
Thyrsis his ewes and Corydon his goats, all udder-
Swollen. Arcadians both, the boys were in their bloom,
Prepared to pair off singing, one and then the other.   5
While I was sheltering my tender myrtles from
The cold, my bully billy strayed away. That's when
I noticed Daphnis, who saw *me* and said, "Come here,
My Meliboeus—quick. Your goat and kids are safe,
So if you can, stop work awhile. Rest here, in shade.   10
Left to themselves to slake their thirst, your kine will steer
Their way to water. Mincius' dark green banks are lined
With canes. The bees come humming from the holy oak."
What could I do? I had no Phyllis or Alcippe
At home to pen the sheep I'd only lately weaned,   15
And Thyrsis versus Corydon—*there* was a match!
Well, surely what they played outweighed my work, I said.
So they began competing with their verse, to sing
In turn—what Muses best remember: alternation.
First Corydon's, then Thyrsis' verses, answering.   20

Corydon:

Libethra's Nymphs, my great delight, grant me the skill

quale meo Codro, concedite (proxima Phoebi
uersibus ille facit) aut, si non possumus omnes,
hic arguta sacra pendebit fistula pinu.

Thyrsis:

Pastores, hedera crescentem ornate poetam, 25
Arcades, inuidia rumpantur ut ilia Codro;
aut, si ultra placitum laudarit, baccare frontem
cingite, ne uati noceat mala lingua futuro.

C:

Saetosi caput hoc apri tibi, Delia, paruus
et ramosa Micon uiuacis cornua cerui. 30
si proprium hoc fuerit, leui de marmore tota
puniceo stabis suras euincta coturno.

T:

Sinum lactis et haec te liba, Priape, quotannis
exspectare sat est: custos es pauperis horti.
nunc te marmoreum pro tempore fecimus; at tu, 35
si fetura gregem suppleuerit, aureus esto.

C:

Nerine Galatea, thymo mihi dulcior Hyblae,
candidior cycnis, hedera formosior alba,
cum primum pasti repetent praesepia tauri,
si qua tui Corydonis habet te cura, uenito. 40

T:

Immo ego Sardoniis uidear tibi amarior herbis,
horridior rusco, proiecta uilior alga,

In song you gave to Codrus (who was next in line
To Phoebus). Or if we can't all possess such power,
I'll hang my clarion pipe up on this holy pine.

Thyrsis:

Shepherds, adorn this rising bard with vines of ivy.   25
Do it, Arcadians, so that Codrus bursts from envy.
Or if I praise too much to please, bind baccar round
My brow—a bard to come whom poison tongues can't wound.

C:

Delia, this little Mico brings a boar's head, bristling—
And ramifying antlers from a long-lived stag.   30
If my luck lasts, then you shall stand in full-length, glistening
Marble, your calves laced up in Punic-crimson buskins.

T:

Cakes and a bowl of milk are all you should expect,
Priapus, every year (you guard a poor man's garden).
For now, we've made you out of marble; if the fold   35
Re-stocks itself with lambs, you'll be a god of gold.

C:

Sweeter than Hybla's thyme, O Nerine Galatea
(Finer than fairest ivy, whiter than a swan):
The very second bulls from pasture find their stalls,
Come fast to Corydon . . . if you love Corydon.   40

T:

By no means let me seem to you more bitter than
Sardinian herbs, meaner than seaweed, rough as broom . . .

si mihi non haec lux toto iam longior anno est.
ite domum pasti, si quis pudor, ite iuuenci.

C:

Muscosi fontes et somno mollior herba,   45
et quae uos rara uiridis tegit arbutus umbra,
solstitium pecori defendite: iam uenit aestas
torrida, iam lento turgent in palmite gemmae.

T:

Hic focus et taedae pingues, hic plurimus ignis
semper, et adsidua postes fuligine nigri.   50
hic tantum Boreae curamus frigora quantum
aut numerum lupus aut torrentia flumina ripas.

C:

Stant et iuniperi et castaneae hirsutae,
strata iacent passim sua quaque sub arbore poma,
omnia nunc rident: at si formosus Alexis   55
montibus his abeat, uideas et flumina sicca.

T:

Aret ager, uitio moriens sitit aëris herba,
Liber pampineas inuidit collibus umbras:
Phyllidis aduentu nostrae nemus omne uirebit,
Iuppiter et laeto descendet plurimus imbri.   60

C:

Populus Alcidae gratissima, uitis Iaccho,
formosae myrtus Veneri, sua laurea Phoebo;

Unless this day is not like one whole year to me.
If you can feel shame, go, my grazing kine; go home.

C:

You mossy springs, and grasses softer still than sleep,   45
And green arbutus roofing you with little shade,
Protect my flock from high-noon sun, for summer comes
A-scorching in; now jewels bud on limbs like jade.

T:

Here is the hearth, with pitch-pine faggots; here, full fire
Always, and doorposts blackened by its constant soot.   50
We care about the Borean cold the way a wolf's
Afraid of sheep, or torrents wish their banks no higher.

C:

Here junipers are standing, and the fuzzy chestnuts
That carpet everything with buckeyes underneath them.
The world is all in smiles. But if the fair Alexis   55
Should leave these hills, you'd see the death of every stream.

T:

In arid acres, thirsty grass and fell miasma.
Liber's denied the hills his shady vines, but at
The advent of our Phyllis, every grove will green,
And Jupiter descend full-strength, in joyous rain.   60

C:

The vines delight Iacchus; poplars, Hercules.
The myrtle's fair to Venus; Phoebus loves his laurel.

Phyllis amat corylos: illas dum Phyllis amabit,
nec myrtus uincet corylos, nec laurea Phoebi.

T:

Fraxinus in siluis pulcherrima, pinus in hortis,   65
populus in fluuiis, abies in montibus altis:
saepius at si me, Lycida formose, reuisas,
fraxinus in siluis cedat tibi, pinus in hortis.

M:

Haec memini, et uictum frustra contendere Thyrsin.
ex illo Corydon Corydon est tempore nobis.   70

While Phyllis loves her hazels—still her favorite trees,
No myrtle nor Apollo's bay outshines those hazels.

T:

In gardens, pine; in forests, ash is fairest tree.   65
Poplars win out by streams, but firs on mountain peaks.
Sweet Lycidas, if you would often come to me,
In woods, the ash would yield to you; in gardens, pine.

M:

So I remember Thyrsis losing, striving on.
Since then, it has been Corydon, all Corydon.   70

Pastorum Musam Damonis et Alphesiboei,
immemor herbarum quos est mirata iuuenca
certantis, quorum stupefactae carmine lynces,
et mutata suos requierunt flumina cursus,
Damonis Musam dicemus et Alphesiboei.   5
tu mihi, seu magni superas iam saxa Timaui
siue oram Illyrici legis aequoris,—en erit umquam
ille dies, mihi cum liceat tua dicere facta?
en erit ut liceat totum mihi ferre per orbem
sola Sophocleo tua carmina digna coturno?   10
a te principium, tibi desinam: accipe iussis
carmina coepta tuis, atque hanc sine tempora circum
inter uictricis hederam tibi serpere lauros.
    Frigida uix caelo noctis decesserat umbra,
cum ros in tenera pecori gratissimus herba: 15
incumbens tereti Damon sic coepit oliuae.

Damon:

Nascere praeque diem ueniens age, Lucifer, almum,
coniugis indigno Nysae deceptus amore
dum queror et diuos, quamquam nil testibus illis
profeci, extrema moriens tamen adloquor hora.   20
    incipe Maenalios mecum, mea tibia, uersus.
Maenalus argutumque nemus pinusque loquentis

ECLOGUE VIII

The pastoral Muse of Damon and Alphesiboeus,
Whose singing stopped the wondering heifer in her grazing;
Whose song the lynxes paused to hear and found amazing;
Whose song stunned rivers in their ever-morphing run:
I'll sing that Muse of Damon's and Alphesiboeus'.   5
But you, my friend, who now cross wide Timavus strewn
With rocks, or skirt Ilyria's coast: when will that day
Ever arrive when I may sing what you have done?
Will that day come when I can tell the world at large
About your songs (alone worth Sophocles' cothurnus)?   10
In you, my true beginning, and in you, my end.
Accept these songs that I began at your command.
Let ivy ring your brows now bound in victory laurels.
The chilly shade of night had barely left the sky
(That's when the dew on tender grass delights the flock),   15
When Damon started, propped up by his olive stock:

Damon:

Lucifer, rise. You bring the world its living light,
While I, deceived in faithless love by Nysa, my
Betrothed, complain. And though the gods have never helped,
I call on them, as in my final hour, I die.   20
    My flute, begin with me a song of Maenalus.
(Whose copses always sing, whose pines speak eloquence).

semper habet, semper pastorum ille audit amores
Panaque, qui primus calamos non passus inertis.
    incipe Maenalios mecum, mea tibia, uersus.   25
Mopso Nysa datur: quid non speremus amantes?
iungentur iam grypes equis, aeuoque sequenti
cum canibus timidi uenient ad pocula dammae.
    incipe Maenalios mecum, mea tibia, uersus.   28a
Mopse, nouas incide faces: tibi ducitur uxor.
sparge, marite, nuces: tibi deserit Hesperus Oetam.   30
    incipe Maenalios mecum, mea tibia, uersus.
o digno coniuncta uiro, dum despicis omnis,
dumque tibi est odio mea fistula dumque capellae
hirsutumque supercilium promissaque barba,
nec curare deum credis mortalia quemquam.   35
    incipe Maenalios mecum, mea tibia, uersus.
saepibus in nostris paruam te roscida mala
(dux ego uester eram) uidi cum matre legentem.
alter ab undecimo tum me iam acceperat annus,
iam fragilis poteram a terra contingere ramos: 40
ut uidi, ut perii, ut me malus abstulit error!
    incipe Maenalios mecum, mea tibia, uersus.
nunc scio quid sit Amor: nudis in cautibus illum
aut Tmaros aut Rhodope aut extremi Garamantes
nec generis nostri puerum nec sanguinis edunt.   45
    incipe Maenalios mecum, mea tibia, uersus.
saeuus Amor docuit natorum sanguine matrem
commaculare manus; crudelis tu quoque, mater.
crudelis mater magis, an puer improbus ille?
improbus ille puer; crudelis tu quoque, mater.   50
    incipe Maenalios mecum, mea tibia, uersus.
nunc et ouis ultro fugiat lupus, aurea durae

His shepherds sing their loves, and Maenalus pays heed,
Hearing out Pan, who first bestirred those latent reeds.
    My flute, begin with me a song of Maenalus.   25
Now Nysa marries Mopsus? Lovers, what to think!
We'll soon see griffins mate with mares; in days to come,
The timid deer will join with hunting dogs to drink.
    My flute, begin with me a song of Maenalus.   28a
Mopsus, cut brand new brands: the bride is brought before you.
Groom, scatter nuts. For you has Hesperus quit Mount Oeta.   30
    My flute, begin with me a song of Maenalus.
Oh, *such* a worthy one you've wed! You scorn the gift
Of every suitor, hating my poor pipe, my goats,
My shaggy brows and bird-nest beard. You act as if
You don't believe that when men sin, the gods take notes.   35
    My flute, begin with me a song of Maenalus.
I was your guide the day I saw you in my garden—
A girl and mother, picking dewy apples. I
Had only reached the age of slightly past eleven,
And barely reached from ground to brittle branches. Oh,   40
I saw; I died. A frenzied madness bore me off.
    My flute, begin with me a song of Maenalus.
I know Love now; Tmarus spawned him on its flint.
Or Rhodope or far-flung Garamantes bore him.
He is a boy not of our kith or kind or kin.   45
    My flute, begin with me a song of Maenalus.
A mother learned from ruthless Love to stain her hands
With her sons' blood. You, too, were cruel, mother. Who
Was crueler, then? The mother or that savage boy?
The boy *was* cruel, but mother, so were you.   50
    My flute, begin with me a song of Maenalus.
Let wolfpacks flee from sheep, and golden apples come

mala ferant quercus, narcisso floreat alnus,
pinguia corticibus sudent electra myricae,
certent et cycnis ululae, sit Tityrus Orpheus,   55
Orpheus in siluis, inter delphinas Arion.
    incipe Maenalios mecum, mea tibia, uersus.
omnia uel medium fiat mare. uiuite, siluae:
praeceps aërii specula de montis in undas
deferar; extremum hoc munus morientis habeto.   60
    desine Maenalios, iam desine, tibia, uersus.
Haec Damon; uos, quae responderit Alphesiboeus,
ducite, Pierides: non omnia possumus omnes.

Alphesiboeus:

Effer aquam et molli cinge haec altaria uitta
uerbenasque adole pinguis et mascula tura,   65
coniugis ut magicis sanos auertere sacris
experiar sensus; nihil hic nisi carmina desunt.
    ducite ab urbe domum, mea carmina, ducite Daphnin.
carmina uel caelo possunt deducere lunam,
carminibus Circe socios mutauit Vlixi,   70
frigidus in pratis cantando rumpitur anguis.
    ducite ab urbe domum, mea carmina, ducite Daphnin.
terna tibi haec primum triplici diuersa colore
licia circumdo, terque haec altaria circum
effigiem duco; numero deus impare gaudet.   75
    ducite ab urbe domum, mea carmina, ducite Daphnin.
necte tribus nodis ternos, Amarylli, colores;
necte, Amarylli, modo et "Veneris" dic "uincula necto."
    ducite ab urbe domum, mea carmina, ducite Daphnin.
limus ut hic durescit, et haec ut cera liquescit   80
uno eodemque igni, sic nostro Daphnis amore.

From iron oaks; from alders, may narcissus bloom.
Let tamarisks sweat thick, rich amber from their bark.
Let swans and owls contend, and Tityrus be Orpheus—   55
An Orpheus in the woods, Arion with the dolphins.
　　My flute, begin with me a song of Maenalus.
May oceans drown the world; live long and prosper, woods!
I'll plummet from the highest summit to the sea.
This is my dying gift; accept it now from me.   60
　　Now end the song of Maenalus, my flute; now end.
So Damon sang. Now you Pierides, say how
Alphesiboeus sang. (We can't *all* do all things.)

Alphesiboeus:

Bring water; tie these altars in the softest rings.
Pile rich vervain and burn the manly frankincense,   65
So I can use these magic rites to change my loved one's
Feelings. Now all I lack are spells and charms and chants.
　　Bring Daphnis home from town, my songs; bring Daphnis home.
For spells can even draw the moon down from the heavens.
Circe used spells to metamorph Ulysses' men.   70
By chanting, we can burst the clammy meadow serpent.
　　Bring Daphnis home from town, my songs; bring Daphnis home.
First, here I tie three different-colored threads around you,
Then circumvent these altars with a little doll
Of you (the god delights in numbers that are odd).   75
　　Bring Daphnis home from town, my songs; bring Daphnis home.
Weave triple knots in triple colors, Amaryllis.
Weave, Amaryllis. Say, "I weave the chains of Venus."
　　Bring Daphnis home from town, my songs; bring Daphnis home.
The way this clay turns hard in flames while wax melts down   80
In the same fire, may Daphnis melt with love for me.

sparge molam et fragilis incende bitumine lauros:
Daphnis me malus urit; ego hanc in Daphnide laurum.
　　ducite ab urbe domum, mea carmina, ducite Daphnin.
talis amor Daphnin qualis cum fessa iuuencum　　　　　　　85
per nemora atque altos quaerendo bucula lucos
propter aquae riuum uiridi procumbit in ulua
perdita, nec serae meminit decedere nocti,
talis amor teneat, nec sit mihi cura mederi.
　　ducite ab urbe domum, mea carmina, ducite Daphnin.　90
has olim exuuias mihi perfidus ille reliquit,
pignora cara sui, quae nunc ego limine in ipso,
Terra, tibi mando; debent haec pignora Daphnin.
　　ducite ab urbe domum, mea carmina, ducite Daphnin.
has herbas atque haec Ponto mihi lecta uenena　　　　　95
ipse dedit Moeris (nascuntur plurima Ponto);
his ego saepe lupum fieri et se condere siluis
Moerim, saepe animas imis excire sepulcris,
atque satas alio uidi traducere messis.
　　ducite ab urbe domum, mea carmina, ducite Daphnin.　100
fer cineres, Amarylli, foras riuoque fluenti
transque caput iace, nec respexeris. his ego Daphnin
adgrediar; nihil ille deos, nil carmina curat.
　　ducite ab urbe domum, mea carmina, ducite Daphnin.
"aspice: corripuit tremulis altaria flammis　　　　　　　105
sponte sua, dum ferre moror, cinis ipse. bonum sit!"
nescio quid certe est, et Hylax in limine latrat.
credimus? an, qui amant, ipsi sibi somnia fingunt?
　　parcite, ab urbe uenit, iam parcite carmina, Daphnis.

Spread meal, and burn the brittle bays with bitumen.
Cruel Daphnis torches me; I burn this bay for him.
    Bring Daphnis home from town, my songs; bring Daphnis home.
May Daphnis feel the love a heifer feels, when worn   85
With searching for her mate in groves and deepest woods,
She kneels beside a stream in verdant sedge, forlorn,
Forgetting she should leave when darkest night appears.
Let him feel love like that—and may I never care.
    Bring Daphnis home from town, my songs; bring Daphnis home. 90
That traitor left me all these trophy trinkets once
As pledges of his love. Earth, take to rest this trash
I hand you, standing in my door; it owes me Daphnis.
    Bring Daphnis home from town, my songs; bring Daphnis home.
These herbs and poison plants he picked in far-off Pontus,   95
Moeris himself has given me (they thrive in Pontus).
With these, I've see him turn to wolf and hide himself
In woods, and often summon spirits from the vasty
Deeps of the grave, and charm sown wheat to fields far off.
    Bring Daphnis home from town, my songs; bring Daphnis home. 100
Take out these embers, Amaryllis; throw them over
Your head and in the river. Don't look back. I'll strike
With these at Daphnis, bored by gods and songs alike.
    Bring Daphnis home from town, my songs; bring Daphnis home.
Look there! All by themselves, while I was dawdling, embers 105
Have blown; the shrine is licked by flame. A sign, from sparks!
Surely there's *something*: Hylax in the doorway barks.
Could it be true? Or are such dreams all lovers' own?
    Stop now, my verses; stop, for Daphnis comes from town.

Lycidas:

Quo te, Moeri, pedes? an, quo uia ducit, in urbem?

Moeris:

O Lycida, uiui peruenimus, aduena nostri
(quod nunquam ueriti sumus) ut possessor agelli
diceret: "haec mea sunt; ueteres migrate coloni."
nunc uicti, tristes, quoniam fors omnia uersat,   5
hos illi (quod nec uertat bene) mittimus haedos.

L:

Certe equidem audieram, qua se subducere colles
incipiunt mollique iugum demittere cliuo,
usque ad aquam et ueteres, iam fracta cacumina, fagos,
omnia carminibus uestrum seruasse Menalcan.   10

M:

Audieras, et fama fuit; sed carmina tantum
nostra ualent, Lycida, tela inter Martia quantum
Chaonias dicunt aquila ueniente columbas.
quod nisi me quacumque nouas incidere lites
ante sinistra caua monuisset ab ilice cornix,   15
nec tuus hic Moeris nec uiueret ipse Menalcas.

ECLOGUE IX

Lycidas:

Moeris on foot? Where to? Taking the path to town?

Moeris:

O Lycidas, to come to this!—a day we never
Conceived could come. A soldier-stranger owns our farm now,
And says, "It's mine; so clear out, all you ancient tenants."
Defeated (all men suffer Fortune's cruel reverses),   5
We're bringing him these goats—to be a flock of curses!

L:

Hadn't I heard that from that place the hills begin to rise,
To where their ridges start to gently slope to water
And ancient beeches with their shivered tops—all this—
Master Menalcas had preserved by singing verses?   10

M:

You did; that's how the rumor ran. But Lycidas,
In Mars's weaponed world, our songs prevail the way
Chaonian doves do with the eagle in a fray.
A left-side raven in a hollow ilex warned me
To break off fighting this new fight, and if he hadn't,   15
No Moeris (or Menalcas either) would have lived.

L:

Heu, cadit in quemquam tantum scelus? heu, tua nobis
paene simul tecum solacia rapta, Menalca!
quis caneret Nymphas? quis humum florentibus herbis
spargeret aut uiridi fontis induceret umbra?   20
vel quae sublegi tacitus tibi carmina nuper,
cum te ad delicias ferres Amaryllida nostras?
"Tityre, dum redeo (brevis est uia), pasce capellas,
et potum pastas age, Tityre, et inter agendum
occursare capro (cornu ferit ille) caueto."   25

M:

Immo haec, quae Varo necdum perfecta canebat:
"Vare, tuum nomen, superet modo Mantua nobis,
Mantua uae miserae nimium uicina Cremonae,
cantantes sublime ferent ad sidera cycni."

L:

Sic tua Cyrneas fugiant examina taxos,   30
sic cytiso pastae distendant ubera uaccae,
incipe, si quid habes. et me fecere poetam
Pierides, sunt et mihi carmina, me quoque dicunt
uatem pastores; sed non ego credulus illis.
nam neque adhuc Vario uideor nec dicere Cinna   35
digna, sed argutos inter strepere anser olores.

M:

Id quidem ago et tacitus, Lycida, mecum ipse uoluto,
si ualeam meminisse; neque est ignobile carmen.
"huc ades, o Galatea; quis est nam ludus in undis?
hic uer purpureum, uarios hic flumina circum   40

L:

My god! Who'd perpetrate a crime like *that?* Menalcas,
You—and your comforting—were nearly snatched from us!
Who'd sing about the Nymphs, or scatter blooming herbs
About the ground? Who'd veil the springs in emerald shadow?   20
Or what about that song I overheard just days
Ago, when you sought out my darling Amaryllis?
"Tityrus, till I'm back (the way's not long), please graze
My goats. And water them, Tityrus, taking care,
In driving them, to watch for Billy Horns; he butts!"   25

M:

Yes, and this song (that's not yet done) he sang to Varus:
"O Varus, spare us Mantua (poor Mantua,
Too near a neighbor to Cremona) and whole choirs
Of swans shall bear your name on high to heaven's stars."

L:

The way you'd want your bees to flee Cyrnean yews;   30
As you'd want clover fodder swelling heifers' udders;
Begin, if you've got lines. The Muses made me, too,
A poet, with my songs. Shepherds say "bard" as well,
But I am not that credulous; I know I still
Can't sing as well as Varius or Cinna can   35
(I'm like a honking goose against the clarion swan).

M:

I mean to, Lycidas; I'm rummaging my mind
To jog my memory (it's no mean composition).
"Come, Galatea; where's the pleasure in those waves?
Here's rosy spring, here streams where Earth has scattered flowers   40

fundit humus flores, hic candida populus antro
imminet et lentae texunt umbracula uites.
huc ades; insani feriant sine litora fluctus."

L:

Quid, quae te pura solum sub nocte canentem
audieram? numeros memini, si uerba tenerem: 45
"Daphni, quid antiquos signorum suspicis ortus?
ecce Dionaei processit Caesaris astrum,
astrum quo segetes gauderent frugibus et quo
duceret apricis in collibus uua colorem.
insere, Daphni, piros: carpent tua poma nepotes."   50

M:

Omnia fert aetas, animum quoque. saepe ego longos
cantando puerum memini me condere soles.
nunc oblita mihi tot carmina, uox quoque Moerim
iam fugit ipsa: lupi Moerim uidere priores.
sed tamen ista satis referet tibi saepe Menalcas.   55

L:

Causando nostros in longum ducis amores.
et nunc omne tibi stratum silet aequor, et omnes,
aspice, uentosi ceciderunt murmuris aurae.
hinc adeo media est nobis uia; namque sepulcrum
incipit apparere Bianoris. hic, ubi densas   60
agricolae stringunt frondes, hic, Moeri, canamus;
hic haedos depone, tamen ueniemus in urbem.
aut si nox pluuiam ne colligat ante ueremur,
cantantes licet usque (minus uia laedit) eamus;
cantantes ut eamus, ego hoc te fasce leuabo.   65

Of every shade. Here silver poplars arch the caves
And pliant vines have woven shady little bowers.
Come here! Let wild waves beat the shores in spumy showers."

L:

And what about those lines I heard you sing alone
On a clear night? What *were* the words (I know the tune)? 45
"Daphnis, why do you watch the stars' eternal risings?
Look there, where Dionean Caesar's comet flashes—
It is a star at which the fields rejoice with grain;
By which the grapes go purple on their sun-shot slopes.
Graft pear trees, Daphnis, so your heirs may pick the fruit." 50

M:

Mere age ends everything—yes, even mind. I know
That as a boy, I'd often set long suns to songs;
Now all my songs are gone. Even his very voice
Abandons Moeris (for the wolves saw Moeris first).
Menalcas, though, will sing them for you—all you wish. 55

L:

By begging off like this, you test my love too much.
Now all the surface of the sea lies still for you.
Look how each breath of murmuring air has fallen off.
From here: our trekking's second half. For I can see
Bianor's tomb from here, just coming into view. 60
Here, hands have stripped dense leaves. Come, Moeris; let us sing.
Here: set the kids down here; we'll get to town no matter.
Or if you fear some rain the evening clouds might bring,
We'll walk right on, and sing (the road won't seem so long).
I'll take your pack so we can carry on with song. 65

M:

Desine plura, puer, et quod nunc instat agamus;
carmina tum melius, cum uenerit ipse, canemus.

M:

No more, lad; let's do what we must. We'll hymn those airs
Much better when their poet-source himself appears.

ECLOGA X

Extremum hunc, Arethusa, mihi concede laborem:
pauca meo Gallo, sed quae legat ipsa Lycoris,
carmina sunt dicenda; neget quis carmina Gallo?
sic tibi, cum fluctus subterlabere Sicanos,
Doris amara suam non intermisceat undam,   5
incipe: sollicitos Galli dicamus amores,
dum tenera attondent simae uirgulta capellae.
non canimus surdis, respondent omnia siluae.
    Quae nemora aut qui uos saltus habuere, puellae
Naides, indigno cum Gallus amore peribat?   10
nam neque Parnasi uobis iuga, nam neque Pindi
ulla moram fecere, neque Aonie Aganippe.
illum etiam lauri, etiam fleuere myricae,
pinifer illum etiam sola sub rupe iacentem
Maenalus et gelidi fleuerunt saxa Lycaei.   15
stant et oues circum; nostri nec paenitet illas,
nec te paeniteat pecoris, diuine poeta:
et formosus ouis ad flumina pauit Adonis.
uenit et upilio, tardi uenere subulci,
uuidus hiberna uenit de glande Menalcas.   20
omnes "unde amor iste" rogant "tibi?" uenit Apollo:
"Galle, quid insanis?" inquit. "tua cura Lycoris
perque niues alium perque horrida castra secuta est."
uenit et agresti capitis Siluanus honore,

ECLOGUE X

For Gallus, grant me one last labor, Arethusa.
For Gallus, I must sing one little poem, Muse—a
Piece Lycoris could read (who'd grudge a song for Gallus?).
If, when you glide below Sicanian streams, you'd flow
Free from the briny waves of Doris mixed with yours,   5
Begin. And let me sing of Gallus' troubled loves
While tender shoots are cropped by snub-nosed nanny goats.
The world I sing to, hears; the trees repeat my notes.
Virgin Naiads, whose woods were those you wandered over
While Gallus perished for a less-than-worthy lover?   10
Neither Parnassus' heights nor Pindus' ridges nor
Aonian Aganippe held you back from him
For whom the laurels wept, and yes, the tamarisks.
Pine-ridged Mount Maenalus ran rills of tears for one
Below a lonely crag; the rocks of cold Lycaeus   15
Cried, too. The sheep stand round, but see in us no shame,
Inspired bard, so you should see no shame in them.
(Even the fair Adonis grazed his flocks by streams.)
The heavy-trudging swineherd came; the shepherd came.
Menalcas came, soaked through from steeping winter mast.   20
All asked where love like this came from. Apollo came,
Demanding, "What's this madness? She you love—Lycoris—
Follows, through snows and through the camps, another man."
Silvanus came and shook his laurelled head bound fast

florentis ferulas et grandia lilia quassans. 25
Pan deus Arcadiae uenit, quem uidimus ipsi
sanguineis ebuli bacis minioque rubentem.
"ecquis erit modus?" inquit. "Amor non talia curat,
nec lacrimis crudelis Amor nec gramina riuis
nec cytiso saturantur apes nec fronde capellae." 30
tristis at ille "tamen cantabitis, Arcades," inquit
"montibus haec uestris; soli cantare periti
Arcades. o mihi tum quam molliter ossa quiescant,
uestra meos olim si fistula dicat amores!
atque utinam ex uobis unus uestrisque fuissem 35
aut custos gregis aut maturae uinitor uuae!
certe siue mihi Phyllis siue esset Amyntas
seu quicumque furor (quid tum, si fuscus Amyntas?
et nigrae uiolae sunt et uaccinia nigra),
mecum inter salices lenta sub uite iaceret; 40
serta mihi Phyllis legeret, cantaret Amyntas.
hic gelidi fontes, hic mollia prata, Lycori,
hic nemus; hic ipso tecum consumerer aeuo.
nunc insanus amor duri me Martis in armis
tela inter media atque aduersos detinet hostis. 45
tu procul a patria (nec sit mihi credere tantum)
Alpinas, a! dura, niues et frigora Rheni
me sine sola uides. a, te ne frigora laedant!
a, tibi ne teneras glacies secet aspera plantas!
ibo et Chalcidico quae sunt mihi condita uersu 50
carmina pastoris Siculi modulabor auena.
certum est in siluis inter spelaea ferarum
malle pati tenerisque meos incidere amores
arboribus: crescent illae, crescetis, amores.
interea mixtis lustrabo Maenala Nymphis 55

With long-stemmed lily flowers and with budding stalks.   25
That god we've often seen ourselves—Arcadia's Pan—
Arrived all smeared blood-red with elderberry juice.
"Will sobbing never cease?" he cried. "Tears don't move Love,
Who's never had his fill of tears—nor grass of rills,
Nor goats of fodder, nor the honeybees of clover."   30
Sad Gallus said, "Arcadians, last of all the master
Singers, you'll chorus still these sorrows to your hills.
Arcadians, oh, how softly then my bones would sleep
If come some day, your pipes would play my loves. And oh,
If only I'd been one of you, guarding your sheep   35
Or working in your vineyards rich with ripened grapes!
I'm certain if Amyntas, Phyllis, or some other
Mad flame (Amyntas is too swarthy? Violets
Are deeply dark, and dark are hyacinths) would lie
With me by sally gardens, under pliant vines,   40
Phyllis would gather garlands, or Amyntas sing.
Lycoris, here are gentle fields, here cold, clear springs.
Woodlands lie here; here only Time would slowly take us.
Now madness in the arms of Mars has gone and placed us
Amid his weapons and the drawn-up enemy.   45
But heartless, far from home, alone and missing me
(Oh, would that I could not believe it), you survey
The frozen Rhine and Alpine snows. Oh, may no blizzards
Harm you, nor jagged ice slice through your tender soles.
I'll go and play, on a Sicilian shepherd's pipe,   50
The songs I first composed once in Chalcidian verse.
I'm sure now that it's better to endure the dens
Of feral beasts and carve on tender trees my love.
Those trees will grow, and as they do, so will my love.
Till then, with Nymphs I'll range all over Maenalus,   55

aut acris uenabor apros. non me ulla uetabunt
frigora Parthenios canibus circumdare saltus.
iam mihi per rupes uideor lucosque sonantis
ire, libet Partho torquere Cydonia cornu
spicula—tamquam haec sit nostri medicina furoris,   60
aut deus ille malis hominum mitescere discat.
iam neque Hamadryades rursus nec carmina nobis
ipsa placent; ipsae rursus concedite siluae.
non illum nostri possunt mutare labores,
nec si frigoribus mediis Hebrumque bibamus   65
Sithoniasque niues hiemis subeamus aquosae,
nec si, cum moriens alta liber aret in ulmo,
Aethiopum uersemus ouis sub sidere Cancri.
omnia vincit Amor: et nos cedamus Amori."
        Haec sat erit, diuae, uestrum cecinisse poetam,   70
dum sedet et gracili fiscellam texit hibisco,
Pierides: uos haec facietis maxima Gallo,
Gallo, cuius amor tantum mihi crescit in horas
quantum uere nouo uiridis se subicit alnus.
surgamus: solet esse grauis cantantibus umbra,   75
iuniperi grauis umbra; nocent et frugibus umbrae.
ite domum saturae, uenit Hesperus, ite capellae.

Or hunt the vicious boars. No winter cold will stop
Me from surrounding with my hounds Parthenius' glens.
I see myself right now by rocks, in sounding groves,
Exulting, shooting from my Parthian bow, Cydonian
Arrows—as if these things could medicine my madness!   60
As if that god could learn to melt at human sorrow!
Again now, neither verse itself nor Hamadryads
Please us. And even now, again you forests leave us.
Our labors work to change the god, but are not able,
Not if we drink the Hebrus' winter water table,   65
Or undergo Sithonian snow and winter sleet.
Not if, when withering bark dies on the tallest elm,
I herd Ethiopian sheep beneath the star of Cancer.
Love conquers all. Let Love then smile at our defeat."
Divine ones: for your poet to have sung these lines   70
While sitting weaving thin hibiscus baskets—that
Will do, Pierides. Make these lines great for Gallus—
Gallus, for whom my love grows greater by the hour,
Or faster than green alders grow in early spring.
Let's rise. For shade can ruin singers. Shadows of   75
The juniper are harmful, and shade kills the grain.
You goats, head home well-fed, for Hesperus comes again.

NOTES

INTRODUCTION

1. The *Eclogues* were probably published circa 37 B.C.E, though individual poems were composed prior to this date; the *Aeneid*, unfinished at the time of his death in 18 B.C.E, was published posthumously.

2. On the Epicurean circle in the Bay of Naples, see the introduction by David Armstrong to *Vergil, Philodemus, and the Augustans*, ed. David Armstrong, Jeffrey Fish, Patricia Johnston, and Marilyn Skinner (Austin: University of Texas Press, 2004).

3. The topic is thoroughly explored in David Halperin, *Before Pastoral: Theocritus and the Ancient Tradition of Bucolic Poetry* (New Haven, Conn.: Yale University Press, 1983).

4. English quotations throughout this introduction are from Len Krisak's translation.

5. Guy Lee, ed., *Virgil: The Eclogues* (Harmondsworth: Penguin, 1984), 45.

6. W. H. Auden, "In Memory of W. B. Yeats," Section II.

7. The English translation is cited from A. S. F. Gow, ed., *Theocritus* (Cambridge: Cambridge University Press, 1950), vol. 1, 90 (my emphasis).

8. For a systematic analysis of the underlying rhetorical strategy of "generic disavowals" (my terminology), see Gregson Davis, *Polyhymnia: The Rhetoric of Horatian Lyric Discourse* (Berkeley: University of California Press, 1991), 28–77.

9. Wendell Clausen, ed., *Virgil: Eclogues* (Oxford: Clarendon, 1994), xv.

TRANSLATOR'S PREFACE

Epigraph: Yehuda Amichai, *Open Closed Open: Poems*, trans. Chana Bloch and Chana Kronfeld (New York: Harcourt, 2000), "Conferences, Conferences: Malignant Words, Benign Speech," 151.

1. Virgil's dactylic hexameters appear here as iambs, with the (conventional) occasional foot-substitution and "promotion" of an ordinarily unstressed syllable.

2. I have had the benefit of consulting many previous translators of the *Eclogues*: George Mackie, J. W. Mackail, H. R. Fairclough, Tony Kline, David Slavitt, David Ferry, and Guy Lee.

ECLOGUE I

1: Samuel Johnson had little respect for the pastoral. Of Milton's "Lycidas," he remarks, "Its form is that of a pastoral, easy, vulgar, and therefore disgusting: whatever images it can supply are long ago exhausted; and its inherent improbability always forces dissatisfaction on the mind" (*Lives of the Poets*).

1.5: "Amaryllis": Most of the proper names Virgil uses are conventional and derived from Theocritus' *Idylls*.

1.6: "one who's like a god to me": presumably a reference to Octavian, returning Tityrus' (Virgil's?) farm to him after the confiscations that followed the battle of Philippi in 41 B.C. We have no way of ascertaining whether the reference to Tityrus' fortune is autobiographical. Blake despised Virgil for lines like this, seeing the deification of the emperor as an abomination. On the other hand, Eliot chided critics for seeing Virgil as "a sycophantic supporter of a middle-class imperialist dynasty" (Russell Kirk, *Eliot and His Age*).

1.11–12: "The land/is crying havoc": Italy is in turmoil after Caesar's assassination, the civil war, and Octavian's settling of farms on de-mobbed soldiers in 41 B.C.

1.27: "Liberty": May be understood either as the personification of the abstract noun or as a goddess.

1.29: "Galatea": not the statue of the Pygmalion story, of course, but simply another conventional name. Galatea is a sea-nymph in Theocritus and elsewhere in the *Eclogues* (7.37; 9.39).

1.32: "I couldn't save . . .": an (ironic?) reference to a Roman slave's inability to own property? Tityrus has often been identified with Virgil; but see note 1.6 above.

1.40: "indentured": more poetic allusiveness on the slavery theme

1.54: "[bees of] Hybla": a Sicilian region famous for its honey

1.58: "Coo with . . . elms": I have tried to honor both Virgil and Tennyson (in his "Princess").

1.61: "vagrant Parthians . . . the Arar": (very) loosely, Persians, seen as eastern nomads; the Arar river (the French Saône) complements, as a western bound; the Parthian tactic of shooting their arrows while in retreat gives us the modern phrase, "Parthian shot."

1.65: "Scythia or the Oaxes": roughly southern Russia; the Oaxes river is unknown. I have followed the Latin from the Loeb edition, "pars Scythiam et rapidum Cretae veniemus Oaxen."

ECLOGUE II

II.1: "Corydon . . . Alexis": both male.

II.21: "the hills of Sicily": a reminder of Virgil's main source, Theocritus, who was from Sicily.

II.23: "Amphion . . . Aracynthus": The son of Jove, Amphion used his lyre to move the stones that built Thebes; Aracynthus is a mountain in Attica, in Greece.

II.24: "Dircean": Amphion warrants the honorific "Dircean" in that he killed Queen Dirce, who had tyrannized his mother.

II.31: "Sylvan Pan": Lines 32 and 33 tell us what we need to know here.

II.46: "Naiads": water nymphs.

II.49: "Mezereon": "casia" (1.49), a shrub with purple flowers.

II.59: "Auster": the South Wind ("blight" because it is hot and dry—the sirocco).

II.61: "Paris": the Trojan shepherd and abductor of Helen, wife of Menelaus and putative cause of the Trojan War.

II.61: "Pallas": Athena (the Roman Minerva), goddess of wisdom; her citadel commands the Acropolis.

II.73: "Another one": Another like Alexis.

ECLOGUE III

III.5–7: "while you . . . like these": As to this "milking" (and the accusations about goats that follow) Virgil leaves the details to the reader's imagination.

III.37: "Alcimedon": This artist/carver remains unknown.

III.40: "Conon . . . who *else*": Our learned shepherd refers to an Alexandrian astronomer and probably to Archimedes, whose accomplishments seem to inform lines 41–42. Both are third-century B.C. historical figures.

III.46: "Orpheus": Legendary Thracian lyre-player whose singing could move stones and trees; retrieving his dead wife Eurydice from the Underworld (on the condition he not look back as she followed), he succumbed to temptation and lost her forever. Maenads later dismembered him, and his singing head floated to Lesbos.

III.59: "the Muses": Originally, the nine goddesses of the poetic arts, all daughters of Mnemosyne ("memory"). Their domain was later expanded to embrace other arts.

III.60: "great Sisters": the Muses again.

III.62: "Phoebus": Phoebus Apollo, god of art, medicine, music, archery, the sun . . . and much else.

III.68: "Venus": the Roman goddess of erotic love.

III.80: "*lupus*": Latin for "wolf"; I have stolen from Auden here.

III.82: "arbutus": strawberry.

III.84: "Pollio" Gaius Asinius Pollio (76 B.C.–A.D. 4), who figures prominently in Eclogues IV and VIII, was a Roman consul and one of Virgil's wealthy benefactors, along with Maecenas.

III.85: "Pierides": the nine Muses, so-called from their home in Pieria, site of Mount Olympus.

III.90: "Bavius . . . Maevius": two unknown poets—and lucky for them, considering Virgil's lines. They may well be fictitious.

III.100: "vetch," a twining legume used to feed livestock.

III.104–105: "Tell me . . . ell": One answer to this clever riddle is available by emailing rereverser@verizon.net.

III.106–107: "And you'll . . . petals": Supposedly, the hyacinth sprang from the blood of either the Homeric Ajax or Hyacinthus, the Spartan prince beloved of Apollo. The petals appear to be marked by what look like the letters AI in Greek—an abbreviation for Ajax: AIAS.

ECLOGUE IV

IV: From as early as the Council of Nicaea (325), this Eclogue, which hails the return of a new Golden Age, has been interpreted, especially in the Middle Ages, as a prediction of the birth of Christ. In Yeats' "Two Songs from a Play," the Roman Empire "stood appalled" when Mary—"that fierce virgin . . . called" (lines 15–16).

IV.1: "Sicilian Muses": Virgil reminds us that Theocritus, whose *Idylls* are a major source of the *Eclogues*, was born in Sicily.

IV.3: "a leader": Pollio (see the note for III.84).

IV.4–6: "The final age . . . regnum": See the introductory note above.

IV.6–7: "Iam redit et virgo . . . / iam nova . . . alto.": These two lines appear (botched) in the Wakefield Pageants' *First Shepherds' Play*, spoken by the First Shepherd. The reach of the medieval church's messianic reading of this poem was truly long.

IV.8: "Lucina": Roman goddess of childbirth.

IV.9: "a *gens*": a line (*gens*) or family hoped to be the descendants of the union of Antony and Octavia (Octavian's sister)—according to one plausible identification of the child.

IV.17: "his father's virtues": presumably Antony's.

IV.20: "colocasia": the Egyptian bean plant.

IV.24: "Death, even for the snake": In Christian interpretations of the poem, the Virgin Mary's crushing of Satan, the serpent, through Christ's birth and sacrifice.

IV.30–31: "yet man's . . . linger": apologies to Milton

IV.32: "Thetis": a sea nymph; roughly, the sea

IV.34: "another Tiphys . . . *Argo*": the helmsman of the *Argo*, the ship that carried Jason and his adventurers to the golden fleece. Lines 34–36 are echoed in Yeats' "Two Songs from a Play," lines 9–12.

IV.42: "lies of varied dyes": "lies" presumably because undyed fabrics would be more "natural," and hence more "honest."

IV.44: "raddled murex": Raddle is red ochre and murex (highly prized in antiquity) is the purple dye of the shell of the mussel.

IV.49: "child of Jove": The newborn's descent is traced from the father of the gods down through Antony, the putative descendant of Hercules, Jove's son.

IV.55: "Linus": a mythical musical shepherd.

IV.57: "Calliope . . . Linus": a paraphrase: "Even if Apollo aided Linus and Calliope helped Orpheus, they would not defeat me in singing these praises." Apollo is god of the arts and Calliope the Muse of heroic epic.

IV.58–59: "Pan . . . Arcadia . . . judging": The Latin here, "Pan etiam, Arcadia mecum si judice certet, / Pan etiam Arcadia dicat se judice victum," clearly requires patterned repetition in English. Pan was the half-goat, half-human deity of herdsmen and the inventor of the pan-pipe, or syrinx. Arcadia, in mountainous central Greece, in the Peloponnese, was the home of Pan in myth and cult. In the later (post-Virgilian) pastoral tradition, Arcadia was transformed into a symbol of an idyllic, irenic existence; Sidney's book-length poem *Arcadia* is instructive.

IV.61: "Ten lengthy months": Latin: *decem*.

IV.62: I have followed the Latin from the Loeb edition, "incipe, parve puer, cui non risere parentes."

ECLOGUE V

V.6: "Zephyr": the balmy West Wind.

V.20: "Daphnis": Born of Mercury and a nymph, he became a shepherd famed for his song. Here he serves as one of the *Eclogues'* many legendary proto-musician-poet figures.

V.28: "Punic": Carthaginian; The site of ancient Carthage lies in present-day Tunisia.

V.29: "Armenian": Armenia lies between the Caspian and Black Seas.

V.30: "Bacchic chorus": the rites of the god of wine and religious ecstasy, also called Dionysus. The son of Zeus and Semele, he led his followers (especially women) in orgiastic mountain frenzies that included torchlight dances and animal dismemberment.

V.31: "around . . . entwines": The god's cult featured the *thyrsus*, a rod wrapped in vine leaves and ivy and topped by a pine cone.

V.35: "Pales: the Roman goddess of flocks and shepherds.

V.45–47: "Celestial . . . stream": Although these lines allude to similar ones in Theocritus' first Idyll, they could be ironic. Does Mopsus' song put Menalcas to sleep because of its soothing or soporific qualities?

V.54: "Stimichon": identity unclear; perhaps Mopsus'"master"?

V.64: "'He is a god. A god, Menalcas'": a deliberate echo of Eclogue 1.7

V.70: "Ariusian": a vintage from the Greek island of Chios

V.78: "Ceres": the goddess of grain; hence the farmers' vows; also called Demeter.

V.86–87: "'The shepherd . . . Meliboeus's'": These are the opening lines of Eclogues II and III respectively.

ECLOGUE VI

VI.2: "Thalia": the Muse of comedy.

VI.2: "verse from Syracuse": Theocritus' (pastoral) dactylic hexameter.

VI.3: "the Cynthian": Apollo, echoing his advice to Callimachus in that poet's *Aitia*.

VI.6: "Varus": Publius Alfenus Varus, one-time general (and consul in 39 B.C.).

VI.14: "Silenus": a Satyr (half-goat, half-man); a toper and a tutor to Bacchus.

VI.15: "Iacchus": another name for Bacchus; roughly, as here, wine.

VI.26: "some other prize": Silenus is a Satyr, so Virgil leaves this "prize" to our imaginations.

VI.29: "Parnassus' cliffs": the slopes of Apollo's mountain at the shrine of Delphi, Apollo being the god of the arts and the symbol of the attainment of artistic immortality through excellence.

VI.30: "Rhodope or Ismarus": Thracian mountains (Thrace because it was the homeland of Orpheus).

VI.36: "Nereus": sea-god father of the sea-nymphs called Nereids.

VI.41: "Saturn's reign": This mini-paean, or hymn-like passage, covers cosmology, myth, and the history of the world, including the Golden Age of Saturn, father of Jove.

VI.41: "Pyrrha": After a great flood, Pyrhha (and Deucalion) repopulated the earth by casting over their shoulders stones that grew into people.

VI.42: "Caucasus' ... Promethean theft": For stealing fire from the gods to give to humankind, Prometheus was chained to a crag in the Caucasus mountains. An eagle (the bird symbol of Jove) came to feed on his liver each day.

VI.43: "Hylas": Hercules' boy on the crew of Jason's *Argo*, drowned in a pool; Virgil, in a show-off effect, has "Hylan," "'Hyla,'" and "'Hyla'" all in two lines. I fear I may have over-adhered to this phonetically marked language in my translation.

VI.45: "Pasiphaë": wife of King Minos of Crete; impregnated by a bull, she gave birth to the monstrous Minotaur.

VI.48: "Proetus' daughters": Punished by Juno for their pride, they were made to believe they were cows.

VI.60: "Gortyn's stalls": Gortyn was a town in Crete (home of the Minotaur).

VI.61: "her whom Hesperidean apples stunned": Hippomenes won Atalanta's hand in a footrace by throwing golden apples (of the Hesperides, the far western isles) in her path (she stopped to pick them up, and so lost the race).

VI.62: "the sibs of Phaëthon ... alders": When Phaëthon crashed his sun-god father's chariot into the earth and died in flames, his sisters wept so copiously that they turned into trees.

VI.64: "Gallus by ... Permessus ... Aonian heights": Gaius Cornelius Gallus (69–26 B.C.), love elegist, soldier, and friend of Augustus and Virgil; the "Sister" is the Muse, who leads him (in these lines, at least) from Permessus (a lowly stream at the foot of Mount Helicon, it symbolizes love poetry) to the Aonian (i.e., Boeotian) heights of more "elevated" verse. Of all Gallus' work, one pentameter survives. He committed suicide at Augustus' hint, possibly on suspicion of disloyalty.

vi.67: "Linus": son of Apollo and tutor to Orpheus (see note on iv.55).

vi.70: "Ascrean bard": Hesiod (ca. 700 b.c.), from the Boeotian town of Ascra, was one of the very earliest Greek poets, author of the *Theogony* and *Works and Days*.

vi.72: "Grynean grove": Gallus apparently wrote a poem about this site in Asia Minor.

vi.74: "Nisus' Scylla": Some confusion may obtain here. Scylla the daughter of King Nisus of Megara was turned into a sea-bird after betraying her father and her city. Scylla at the Straits of Messina was the famous mariners' monstrous peril. For the first Scylla, see Ovid, *Metamorphoses*, Book viii.

vi.76: "Dulichian": Dulichium was a small island near Odysseus' homeland of Ithaca. His ship faced the peril of Scylla the monster in Homer's *Odyssey*.

vi.78–79: "Tereus' limbs . . . Philomel's cooked offerings": Raped (and her tongue cut out) by her brother-in-law Tereus, Philomela and her sister Procne got revenge by killing Tereus' son Itys and serving him to his unsuspecting father. Ovid in *Metamorphoses*, Book vi, tells how Philomela became a nightingale and Tereus turned into a hoopoe.

vi.83: "Eurotas": Spartan river, site of the accidental death-by-discus of Apollo's beloved Hyacinthus—by the god's own hand.

vi.85: "Vesper": Hesperus, the evening star.

ECLOGUE VII

vii.12: "Mincius'": The river Mincio runs through Virgil's birthplace of Mantua.

vii.18–20: "So they began . . . answering": The Muses are the daughters of Memory (Mnemosyne), and matching alternate verses, by the same rationale offered for modern poetic meter and rhyme, would make them easier to remember than random lines.

vii.21: "Libethra's Nymphs": roughly, the Muses, since Libethra is a town near Mount Olympus, where Orpheus was buried, according to local legend.

vii.22: "Codrus": the last king of Athens.

vii.27: "baccar": a fragrant-rooted plant; perhaps cyclamen (see Eclogue iv, line 19.).

VII.33: "Priapus": a fertility god of the Italian countryside; his statue featured a phallus.

VII.37: "Nerine Galatea": The first Galatea was a sea-nymph, or Nereid, hence "Nerine."

VII.51: "Borean": Boreas is the North Wind.

VII.58: "Liber": yet another name for Bacchus.

VII.64: "Apollo's bay": The tree sacred to the god is the laurel, often associated with the common bay.

VII.69: "Thyrsis losing": Just in what way is difficult to say, since translation seriously complicates the issue. Is Thyrsis' Latin verse bad, mediocre, or (ironically) good?

ECLOGUE VIII

VIII.2: "wondering heifer": not a typo for "wandering," but a pun; The Latin is *mirata*.

VIII.6: "you, my friend . . . Illyria's coast": Pollio again; poet and soldier, he crossed the Timavus river in Illyria during his campaign against the Parthini in 39 B.C. Illyria was roughly the recent nation-state of Yugoslavia.

VIII.10: "Sophocles' cothurnus": quite a compliment; Virgil compares Pollio's writing to that of the great Greek dramatist. The cothurnus, or buskin, was a high boot worn by tragic actors.

VIII.17: "Lucifer": the morning star; in Latin, "light-bearer."

VIII.21: "Maenalus": a mountain in Arcadia associated with the god Pan.

VIII.31: "scatter nuts": a Roman wedding custom.

VIII.31: "Mount Oeta": a mountain in Thessaly. When Hesperus, the evening star, has left the mountain peak, the (evening) wedding begins.

VIII.44: "Tmarus": a mountain in Epirus.

VIII.45: "Garamantes": a distant African tribe.

VIII.48–49: "A mother . . . mother": Medea, who to revenge herself on Jason for his desertion of her, murdered their two sons.

VIII.50: "that savage boy": Cupid, than whom, who is crueler?

VIII.57: "Arion": a poet thrown overboard but safely returned to Corinth by rescuing dolphins. His invention of the dithyramb (a choral song to the god Dionysus) is connected with the beginnings of Greek tragedy.

VIII.71: "Circe . . . Ulysses' men": in Homer's *Odyssey*, the witch-sorceress who turns Ulysses' men into animals.

VIII.81: "The way ... for me": sympathetic magic.

VIII.96: "Pontus": the Black Sea, a region associated in classical times with Medea, poison, and witchcraft.

VIII.108: "Hylax": Greek for "barker."

ECLOGUE IX

IX.3–4: "A soldier ... tenants": see note to Eclogue 1.6.

IX.13: "Chaonian doves": the doves of the oracle at Dodona in Chaonia, a region of Epirus.

IX.26: "Varus ... Mantua ... Cremona": for Varus, see note to Eclogue VI.6; Mantua (Virgil's birthplace) and nearby Cremona did not fare well in Varus' dispossession of the farmlands mentioned in Eclogue 1.

IX.30: "Cyrnean yews": Corsican trees; *Kyrnos* (Greek) = "Corsica."

IX.35: "Varius or Cinna": A contemporary of Virgil, Gaius Helvius Cinna wrote a learned, esoteric poem, "Zmyrna," and was also a friend of Catullus. For the Roman mob's confusing another Cinna with him, see Shakespeare's *Julius Caesar*. L. Varius Rufus, a friend of Virgil's, was an epic, lyric, and tragic poet.

IX.47: "Dionean Caesar": The mother of Venus, Dione establishes Julius Caesar's descent: Venus → Aeneas → Iulus → the Iulian *gens* or clan → Julius Caesar.

IX.60: "Bianor's tomb": Bianor was the legendary founder of Virgil's hometown of Mantua.

ECLOGUE X

X.1: "Gallus ... Arethusa": For Gallus, see note to Eclogue VI.64. Arethusa was the nymph of a Sicilian spring. Here she more or less stands in for the Muse of pastoral poetry.

X.3: "Lycoris": Gallus' (pseudonymous) mistress.

X.4: "Sicanian": Sicilian; see note for line 1 above.

X.5: "Doris": wife of Nereus; roughly, the sea.

X.11: "Pindus' ridges": mountain range between Thessaly and Macedonia associated with the Muses.

X.12: "Aonian Aganippe": a spring on Mount Helicon; Aonia is Boeotia, home of the mountain.

X.15: "Lycaeus": a mountain in Arcadia.

x.18: "Adonis": beautiful young hunter loved by Venus. He died on the tusks of a wild boar.

x.20: "mast": windfall acorns, etc., used for fodder.

x.24: "Silvanus": a forest god of Italy.

x.51: "Chalcidian verse": Chalcis is in Euboea. This may refer to the poet Euphorion of Chalcis, or to elegiac ("Sicilian") verses—a hexameter followed by a pentameter—adapted to Virgil's pastoral hexameter (of six feet).

x.57: "Parthenius": a mountain in Arcadia.

x.59–60: "Cydonian/Arrows": Cydonia was a town in Crete whose inhabitants were noted for their archery.

x.62: "Hamadryads": nymphs or dryads came in all types, for all occasions. Hamadryads are wood nymphs.

x.65: "the Hebrus": a Thracian river.

x.66: "Sithonian [snow]": Sithonia is a Thracian peninsula.

x.68: "the star of Cancer": the zodiacal sign of the crab; roughly, "under torrid conditions."